How to Make Your Own

Brewskis

How to Make Your Own Brewskis

Mark Murphy &
Jordan St. John

...THE GO-TO GUIDE FOR CRAFT BREW ENTHUSIASTS

BARRON'S

First edition for the United States and Canada in 2012 by
Barron's Educational Series, Inc.

Editorial Director: Will Steeds
Consultants: Graham Lees and Jon Downing
Project Editors: Laura Ward and Judith John
Cover and Interior Design: Lindsey Johns
Illustrator: Robert Brandt

All inquiries should be addressed to:
Barron's Educational Series, Inc.
250 Wireless Boulevard, Hauppauge, New York 11788
www.barronseduc.com

ISBN: 978-1-4380-0170-8

Library of Congress Control No. 2012943881

Printed in China

9 8 7 6 5 4 3 2 1

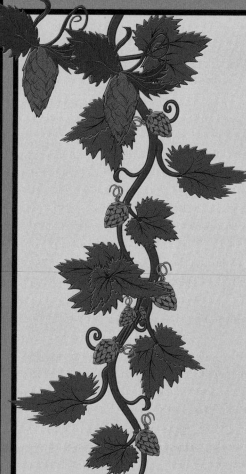

Introduction 6

Chapter 1: What You Will Need 8

Chapter 2: The Brewing Process 38

Chapter 3: The Easy Brew Method 64

Chapter 4: Belgian Wit 76

Chapter 5: California Common 88

Chapter 6: Porter 100

Chapter 7: IPA (India Pale Ale) 112

Glossary 126

Acknowledgments 128

Introduction

Have you ever pondered just what goes into making a good beer? Or wondered whether you could make a brew just like your favorite one in the bar or from the store?

Well, this illustrated guide answers both those questions—and much more.

Brewskis shows you what goes into your favorite tipple and how it's made—and provides you with some lip-smacking recipes to work on yourself.

Brewskis is a step-by-step manual not just to making good beer, but to making excellent beer. We take you through the whole brewing journey, from detailing the ingredients and the equipment you will need, and the processes leading to a fine frothing finish in your glass.

Whether you want to make a simple brew to start with, using the bare basics, or you feel ready to tackle a more sophisticated beer with a few exotic ingredients, such as spicy coriander seed and orange peel, we'll guide you through each step of the process.

We've written *Brewskis* in as non-technical a style as possible but, where we can't avoid a few technical terms, there's a handy glossary toward the end of the book to explain these in everyday terms, to help you feel like a professional brewer.

Making beer isn't expensive—in fact, it'll save you $$$s on your bar bill—and it's a lot of fun. Plus, it'll be a great point of conversation when you invite a few pals around to sample what you've produced.

So, what are you waiting for? Let's get started!

Jordan St. John & Mark Murphy

About the Authors

Jordan St. John is a Canadian beer writer, blogger, brewer, and student at Canada's first-ever brewing program at Niagara College. He lives in Toronto, Ontario, and periodically does things that aren't even related to beer.

Mark Murphy was a homebrewing accountant before he took his hobby to the next level by pursuing a professional brewing education. He enjoys hop puns, beer festivals, and the occasional glass of beer.

Chapter 1

What You Will Need

This chapter will guide you through the chief ingredients of beer and the equipment you will need to make a good brew. There are four basic ingredients: water, barley, hops, and yeast. However, brewers often add other stuff—such as wheat malt, or rice, or herbs, even spices such as coriander—but here we'll focus on the fundamentals.

Water

Whichever type of beer you brew, and whatever strength it has, it will always be at least 90 percent water. It seems like an innocuous ingredient but good ol' H_2O plays an incredibly important role in the quality of your home brew. Most of the flavor in your beer will come from the malt, hops, and yeast you use; but in order to make sure it turns out well you need to get your water right, too.

The first thing to do is to taste the water that you'll be using. If you wouldn't drink the water that comes out of your faucet, you probably shouldn't be brewing with it—or at least not without some modification. If the local water has a distinctive mineral or sulphuric taste, it will carry through into your beer. If that's the case, your water is probably not suited to brewing.

Chlorination

Another significant water problem is chlorination. Many suppliers add chlorine to their water as a purification agent. This ensures that microorganisms can't survive in the water. The problem is that chlorinated water can lead to unpleasant flavor compounds called chlorophenols in your finished beer.

These compounds tend to have a vaguely medicinal smell not unlike a new band aid.

Fortunately, the removal of chlorine is a relatively straightforward process. If you have a water filtering system that you're already using for drinking water, it's not unfeasible to run a few gallons of water through it. For larger volumes, however, you need a less time-consuming method.

The simplest method is to use Campden tablets. These will remove chlorine and chloramines from the water that you're using by adding sulfur dioxide to the mix. Campden tablets will also kill off any bacteria that could inhibit yeast growth during your fermentation. A single Campden tablet will prove effective for up to 20 gallons (76 L) of brewing water, about four batches of beer.

Water Treatment

The name "Campden," in case you're wondering, comes from the small town of Chipping Campden in Gloucestershire, England, where the compound was developed by scientists in the 1920s.

Campden Tablets

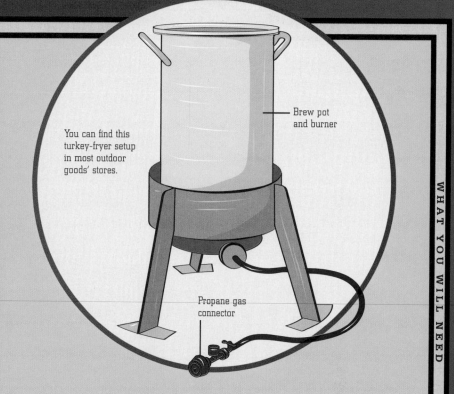

You can find this turkey-fryer setup in most outdoor goods' stores.

Brew pot and burner

Propane gas connector

You also want all of the water that comes into contact with your equipment during the brewing process to be chlorine free.

Another option is boiling the water that you're going to use for the entire brewing process. This is more labor intensive, however.

Water Sources

If you've read much about the different beers of the world, one of the things you'll have noticed is how those beer styles originated. They were heavily influenced by the local ingredients at hand—not least of which being the water type.

There are entire books written about the characteristics of water in famous brewing cities, and how they've influenced the character of the local beer styles. Although it's always good to try to copy the masters, for your purposes it's going to be difficult to replicate those characteristics exactly with minimal equipment.

The best thing to do is visit your city's website and locate a water report for the municipality. You're looking for two things: calcium and magnesium content. The presence of both of these minerals is required in order to get the starch in your grain to convert into the sugar that your yeast will feed on. Zinc content is also important to help the yeast.

If you decide that you just can't trust your local water supply, you should consider buying large quantities of bottled water. But you still need to pay attention to that water's mineral content. The good news is that since bottled water tends to be low in mineral content, you can add gypsum to your water.

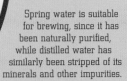

Spring water is suitable for brewing, since it has been naturally purified, while distilled water has similarly been stripped of its minerals and other impurities.

Grains

You'll want your beer to be of good quality, but there's no need to adopt the strictures of the 500-year-old Bavarian purity law still used by German brewers as a brewing standard.

That law, in German *das Reinheitsgebot*, insists that only barley malt can be used in brewing. It was enforced to make sure brewers didn't cheat drinkers by using inferior ingredients. (At the time it was created, some brewers were slinging all manner of "fermentables" into their mix, including dead sheep.)

Today, brewers mix different grains, including rice, corn, wheat, oats, and rye, although barley remains the staple basic fermentable ingredient. Some brewers are now making gluten-free beers, using sorghum or brown rice.

Ear of corn

Wheat is the most commonly used grain behind barley, since it contributes proteins which aid in head (beer foam) retention.

Barley Malt

The recipes in this book will focus on barley malt. This is because your home brew should, ideally, feature the best possible ingredients. If you didn't want flavor, you'd be buying cases of light beer instead of making your own beer.

Malt is grains which have been treated in a process known as malting. Dried grain is induced to germinate by soaking it in water. That process is then halted by drying the grains with hot air.

This develops the enzymes required to modify the grain's starches into sugars, which your yeast will devour and convert into alcohol. (You like alcohol, right? Of course you do.)

There are two basic varieties of barley malt used in brewing: two-row barley and six-row barley. These are terms which refer to the shape and size of the barley "ear" where the grains are formed. Because the recipes in this book are ales, we're going to be focusing on two-row barley, which usually has more fermentable sugar content. (Six-row barley is mostly used for lagers.)

Unmalted barley

The barley has been soaking in water and is beginning to germinate and sprout.

Two-row barley has plumper kernels and therefore more fermentable sugar content.

Six-row barley has higher enzyme levels and is more commonly used in American-style lagers, where adjuncts are used.

14

Beer Color

When you mash your grains, what you're doing is restarting the enzymatic action that releases sugar from the barley.

There are several ways of malting barley to create different flavors. The amount of heat and moisture applied to the grains, and the period of time they are "cooked" in the malting before the treatment is halted, influences malt flavor.

The lighter in color a malt is, the more likely it will be a major contributor to the fermentable material in your recipe, but it doesn't contain a great deal of flavor and it doesn't give your beer a lot of color.

The color of beer is almost entirely imparted by the way malt is prepared, and it's measured on a scale called the "Standard Reference Method." The Belgian Witbier recipe in this book is going to be the lightest in color. At three on the scale, it's going to be very light, slightly lighter than the color of dried straw. The next lightest will be the California Common, followed by the IPA (India Pale Ale). The Porter recipe is going to be about thirty-three on the scale and will be practically opaque—dark brown, leaning toward black.

The darker in color a malt ingredient is, the more flavorful it will be in the context of your recipe. It will also contain less convertible starch. You couldn't expect to make a beer using all-black malt, because there's just not much there to ferment. Also, it would impart a burned taste. It's a question of proportion. You might want some of the color and character of black malt, but you might not want it to make up more than the three percent of the total malt used.

The Standard Reference Method Chart

The Standard Reference Method (SRM) is one method by which brewers measure beer color. Using a specific wavelength, light is passed through the beer and the light absorption of the liquid is measured. On the home brew scale, online beer recipe calculators will determine the color for you, based on the grains you are using. Hold your glass of beer up to a light and compare it with the chart here to see how close the calculations are to your end result.

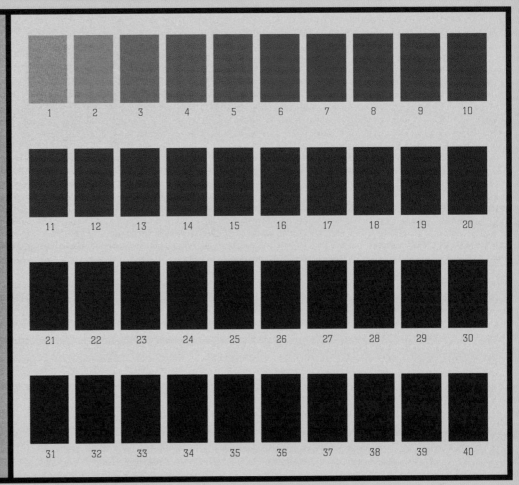

Hops

Due to the number of IPAs (India Pale Ales) being produced in North America, hops have become the most glamorous ingredient. Hops are closely related to hemp, or cannabis—but they don't share any of the psychoactive properties! (So you can put your bong down, Cheech.)

Hops provide flavor and aroma, they act as a preservative, and they help maintain the foamy head on your beer. They are perennial plants, meaning that they grow back year after year. They're generally quite hardy and tend to be grown in temperate climates which have cold winters. This helps explain why some of the major beer styles have their roots in central Europe, which is home to two of the most famous hop-growing regions—the Hallertau in southern Germany, and Zatec in Bohemia in the Czech Republic, home of Saaz hops.

Growing up a trellis, hops can reach over 20 feet (6 m) in height.

While there are styles of beer that are obviously a great deal hoppier than others, even a light beer with a very mild flavor will contain hop bitterness in some proportion. The flavor of your beer will be influenced by hops at nearly every stage, whether they are added at the beginning of the boil for bitterness, or toward the end of the boil for aroma.

It's fairly unlikely that you'll be using hop cones in your home brewing. All of the oils and resin that brewers are interested in are in a part of the cone called the lupulin gland; the rest of a hop cone is more or less redundant plant matter that will just take up room in your kettle.

Cross-section of a hop cone showing the yellow lupulin glands.

So, hops for home brewing are best in a pelletized form—hop cones milled down to a state where they're more easily handled. The pellets also contain vegetative matter, but instead of dealing with whole leaves from a cone, you're dealing with tiny specks of those leaves. Hop pellets should be kept in oxygen-free bags in cold storage. They can last up to over a year in your fridge without deteriorating much.

When you buy hop pellets, the information on the package will include the variety of hop and the weight of the package. But what you're most interested in for brewing is the percentage of alpha acids (AA) that the hops contain.

To the untrained eye, hop pellets could be taken for rabbit food; bunny won't like 'em.

Hop bitterness

Hop bitterness is measured in IBUs, or International Bitterness Units. Each style of beer has a different hop profile, both in terms of the varieties and in the amount of bitterness. For example, a light lager might contain around ten IBUs and be barely detectable, while a Double IPA might reach the theoretical saturation point of 110 IBUs. Therefore, knowing the percentage of alpha acids is important.

For example, if your recipe includes an ounce (28 g) of Hallertauer hops at 4 percent alpha acid, and the hops you bought contain 3 percent alpha acid, you're going to need to adjust the amount of hops you include in the recipe upward. Similarly, if your Hallertauers contain 5 percent alpha acid, you'll have to scale the amount down a little.

Hop Varieties and Their Bitterness Levels

Hop varieties have been bred to thrive in their local growing conditions, but also to promote certain characteristics, such as alpha acid levels, disease resistance, and aroma compounds.

Hop Variety	Alpha Acid % Range	Characteristics
Amarillo	8–11%	Citrusy and floral
Cascade	4.5–7%	Very aromatic and great for dry hopping
Chinook	12–14%	Spicy, piney, and grapefruit aromas
East Kent Golding	4–5.5%	Gentle, fragrant, and pleasant. Common English hop
Fuggle	4–5.5%	Mild, woody, and fruity. Typical English aroma hop
Hallertau	3.5–5.5%	Slightly flowery and spicy. Traditional German aroma hop
Saaz	3–4.5%	Spicy and earthy
Simcoe	12–14%	Piney aroma

Yeast

There are many different types of yeast, but for brewing there are only two kinds: lager yeast and ale yeast. They both have long scientific names, and are separate species: *Saccharomyces Carlsbergensis* (lager yeast) and *Saccharomyces Cerevisiae* (ale yeast). *Saccharomyces* translates very simply as "sugar fungus," which is exactly accurate: it's a fungus that eats sugar. Not only does yeast eat sugar, but it turns that sugar into carbon dioxide and alcohol.

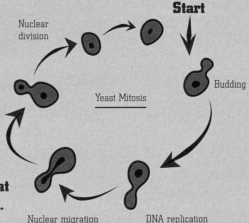

Start

Nuclear division

Budding

Yeast Mitosis

Nuclear migration

DNA replication

Ale Yeast

Ale yeast has been part of human civilization for thousands of years. In addition to being used in beer, it's also used to make bread. Granted, the yeast that you use in bread is a slightly different strain from the one you would use to make beer, but it's the same species. Ale yeast generally does best at room temperature, but can usually function between 55 and 75°F (13 and 24°C) without problem.

When introduced to your wort in the fermenter, ale yeast will take a little while to acclimatize and begin to feed on the sugars. This is called the "lag phase," and it's at this point that the yeast is consuming vitamins, minerals, amino acids, and oxygen in order to begin reproducing. As soon as it starts reproducing, it gets very, very busy. By the time you see it doing something, it will have formed a crusty-looking layer of foam on top of the liquid in the fermenter. This is called *krausen*, and it's a very good sign—your yeast is happily reproducing and turning your wort into beer. (It's because of the krausen that ale yeast is known as a top fermenting yeast.)

Ale yeast might take up to seventy-two hours to come out of the lag phase, and it will probably be five or six days before the fermentation is complete. After that, you will need to transfer the brew to your secondary fermentation vessel and allow the

Krausen on top of the fermenting beer

beer to condition. During this period, the remaining yeast in the beer will absorb some diacetyl, a natural by-product of fermentation which creates a buttery taste, and other flavors that you find in very young beer will disappear. The remaining yeast will eventually settle to the bottom of your container. Your ale will generally be finished conditioning in seven to ten days.

Lager Yeast

Lager yeast works slightly differently. It thrives at lower temperatures than ale yeast. If you use lager yeast to ferment a lager-style beer, aim for between 45 and 55°F (7 and 14°C) for the initial fermentation.

Secondary fermentation takes place at a much lower temperature, ideally somewhere between 38 and 45°F (3–7°C). It also goes on for longer.

Ales are noted for their fruity yeast aromas, or esters, and these are backed up by the residual sugars in the finished beer. Lager yeast tends to eat up more of the fermentable material, but this process slows down toward the end of the fermentation process. Very young lagers will often have a period where there are flavors that you wouldn't want in a finished beer: sulphurous compounds and diacetyl (which imparts a buttery kind of character, as mentioned earlier). These problems are solved by the process of "lagering"—aging the beer for three to four weeks.

The difference in conditioning time and the additional resources needed to ferment a lager properly are probably the reason that the majority of home brewers prefer to brew ales.

THE BASIC KIT

The trusty glass carboy, centerpiece of the home brewer's kit.

Now that we've assessed what's likely to go into your beer, let's look at the equipment you'll need to produce it and how it works. The basic kit usually consists of a fermenting pail (or a glass carboy), an airlock, a hydrometer, a racking cane, and a bottle filler.

Malted grain brewing requires more equipment than you might have used in trying malt extract kits, but it needn't be expensive. Chances are that you'll be able to source some of it via craigslist.com, the online second-hand goods site. If not, visit a home brew store.

We'll explain all the options open to you, including brewing small or large beer batches, and the pros and cons of each item of equipment. You may not have the space for a full 5-gal. (19 L) batch if you're living in a small apartment, in which case you can brew 1-gal. (4 L) batches with only slight modifications to the equipment needed.

Mashing Equipment

With grain brewing you'll need equipment for mashing, which is the single most important part of the process. If you're working with a 5-gallon (19 L) batch, you'll need a vessel—your mash tun in brewing lingo—able to hold up to 10 lbs (4½ kg) of grain and a significant amount of water. The receptacle you choose will need to be sufficiently insulated to keep the temperature of your mash constant.

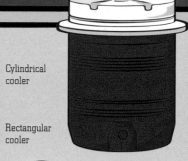

Cylindrical cooler

Rectangular cooler

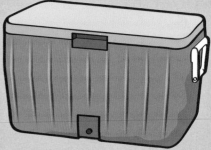

Mash Tuns

For a one-gallon (4 L) brew, your mash tun could be a 2-gal. (7½ L) pot. The good news is that if you've ever made pasta, you've probably got one of these kicking around your kitchen. You'll also need a way to sparge the grain you've mashed in the pot. Since it's a fairly small amount of soaked grain, you might be able to use something as simple as a mesh bag or a fine mesh kitchen colander. The technique is called, unsurprisingly, "brew in a bag," and sparging in this case is the action of slowly lifting the bag in and out of the pot. But for five gallons or more, it's not advisable to attempt the "brew in a bag" method. Wet grain is heavy, and you'll never be exactly sure of the strength of your bag.

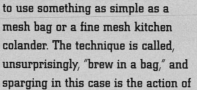

Fine mesh kitchen colander

The easiest and cheapest way to build a proper mash tun is to convert a plastic beverage cooler, which has the added benefit of being insulated to maintain your mash temperature. Mash tuns can be made out of either cylindrical or rectangular coolers.

You'll need the kind of cooler that has a drain plug at the bottom to enable you to put in some steel mesh tubing, and a valve that will let you control the outflow of liquid. For 5-gal. (19 L) batches, a 5-gal. (19 L) cylindrical cooler or 24-quart (23 L) rectangular cooler works best.

You are looking for a grain bed depth of between 6 and 12 inches (15–30 cm). For 10-gal. (38 L) batches, double these sizes. Even if you have to purchase a cooler, the entire outlay should come to just under $50. There are guides on YouTube showing how to convert a cooler into a mash tun, or pay a visit to www.homebrewtalk.com/wiki/index.php/Converting_a_cooler_to_a_mash_tun. It's easier than you'd think.

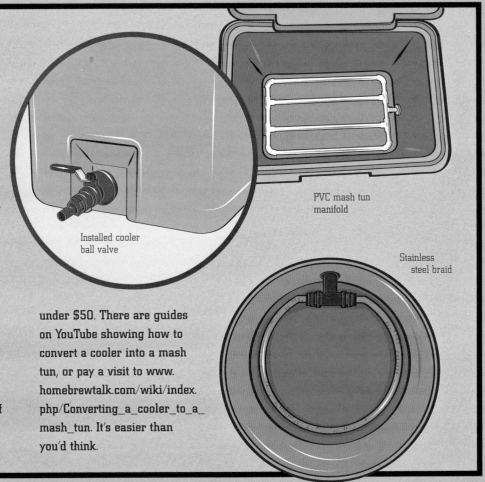

Installed cooler
ball valve

PVC mash tun
manifold

Stainless
steel braid

Mash Paddle

Your mash paddle can be stainless steel or plastic. Sanitation at this point isn't critical, since after the mashing process your wort will be boiling. What is important is for your paddle to be heavy duty, and to have a large enough surface area to mix your wort with a minimum of effort.

Stainless steel mash paddle

Iodine Test Kit

This will tell you whether your mash is mashing. You use it by placing a small sample of wort in a bowl or on a plate. Add a drop of iodine and if it turns a deep purple or black, starch is still present and the mash has not fully converted. Continue mashing for ten minutes and recheck. If the iodine stays a brown color, the mash conversion process is complete.

Be careful not to get any pieces of grain in your sample, since grain husk contains starch and will give you a false reading.

Boiling Equipment

Brew Kettle or Pot

This is needed to actually cook your beer, and it's potentially the most expensive piece of equipment—so it's worth pausing to consider how much beer you plan to brew. The brew pot will be used for mashing, boiling, and sparging, especially if you're using the boil-in-the-bag method (see page 72).

Having an appropriately sized pot goes a long way to preventing boil overs and arguments over the mess you've made in the kitchen.

Consider that brewing on a smaller scale doesn't lead to a significant decrease in the length of your brew day. It will still take an hour to mash, an hour to boil, and altogether between five and eight hours (including preparation and cleaning), regardless of whether you produce one gallon at a time or twenty.

If you plan to brew 1-gal. (4 L) batches, you can manage with a 2-gal. (7½ L) pot. But, in any case, having a pot approximately double your batch size will allow you to heat up all of your brewing and cleaning water, and will help to make sure that the kettle's walls are high enough to keep all of the liquid where it's supposed to be. You can use this pot to heat all of your water for the day, and then transfer the water to other kitchen pots, or even to the fermenter (see page 53) for temporary storage.

Stainless steel brew pot

If you're planning to brew 5-gal. (19 L) batches of beer, you'll probably need to purchase two 8–10-gal. (30–38 L) pots. One pot will act as your hot liquor tank, and the other will be your boil pot.

You could save money by buying a large stock pot from a restaurant supply store, although this won't have the handy spigot on the side. But remember that you might have to move this pot at some point when it contains gallons of very hot liquid, so make sure it has strong handles.

Another option, if you're a DIY type, is to convert a standard half-barrel keg into a "keggle." All you need to do is depressurize the keg, remove the spear inside, and cut the top off, and you've got a 15½-gal. (59 L) brew pot. The good news is that if you're interested in home brewing, you probably already know people who have kegs lying around that they might be willing to part with. There is a wide variety of welded and weldless fittings available online.

An appropriately sized burner or heating source is important, as there's nothing worse than waiting an hour just for your batch of beer to reach a boil. For 1-gal. (4 L) batches,

the kitchen stove is probably sufficient, but for bigger batches you might be advised to move out into the yard or garden. Propane

gas burners are inexpensive, but you could invest in a turkey fryer, which includes the gas burner and a stainless steel pot. Your local home brew store will have a range of burners, although none of them will come with the promise of delicious turkey, too.

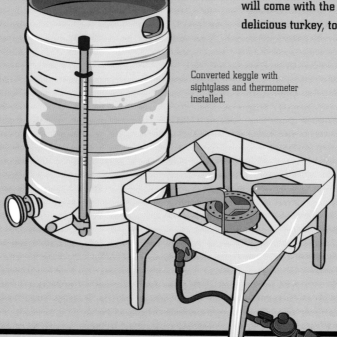

Converted keggle with sightglass and thermometer installed.

Propane gas burners with 60,000+ Btu (18 kW) will get your wort boiling in a jiffy.

Fermenting Equipment

Plastic Bucket or Glass Carboy

These are the two most popular types of fermenters for home brewers. Like the brew kettles, the most important thing is to get the sizing correct. As a general rule, it's best to leave about 20 percent headspace in your fermenter so that the krausen (the foam produced during fermentation) does not get into your airlock. If you brew a 5-gal. (19 L) batch, it's best that you go with a fermenter with a 6-gal. (23 L) capacity.

Food-safe plastic buckets, with airtight lids, are usually less expensive than glass carboys and generally have the added benefit of having a spigot, which comes in handy during the bottling process. Glass carboys are significantly heavier, but have a better seal, which helps during conditioning to prevent oxidation of your beer. Be sure to cover a glass carboy with cloth to prevent sunlight causing unpleasant flavors. A glass carboy also lets you monitor the progress of fermentation.

Plastic:
- Cheaper
- Lighter and shatter resistant
- Not airtight
- Easier to clean, but harder to sanitize (prone to scratching which can encourage bacteria growth)

Glass:
- Heavier
- The use of an airlock will create an airtight seal
- Easier to sanitize
- Breakable and potentially dangerous

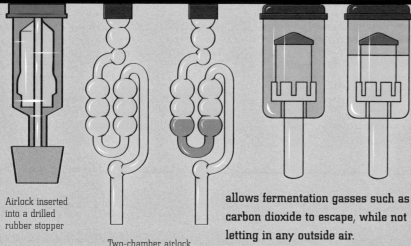

Airlock inserted
into a drilled
rubber stopper

Two-chamber airlock
(with and without water)

Three-piece airlock
(with and without water)

But whether you choose a glass or plastic container, use a non-abrasive scrubber when cleaning, so as not to create scratches where bacteria can grow.

For the fermentation process, you'll need an airlock. The basic airlock is a drilled rubber stopper with a plastic chamber that attaches. The airlock allows fermentation gasses such as carbon dioxide to escape, while not letting in any outside air.

If you've got a slightly larger batch than you had anticipated, you don't necessarily have to pour out some of the liquid. You can use a blow-off hose—a length of tube fitted into a drilled rubber stopper. Use this in place of an airlock during the start of a particularly vigorous fermentation. In order to keep things clean, put the other end of the tube into a glass of sanitizer or water and allow the CO_2 to bubble through it.

Consider, also, buying a yeast starter kit. This will allow you to prepare your yeast up to two days before brew day, which will dramatically increase the performance of the yeast and the quality of your beer. It reduces the lag phase of the yeast and increases the pitching rate to ensure a rapid and complete fermentation. Each kit is slightly different, but they all contain a glass flask and dry malt extract. Follow the kit's directions.

Measuring Equipment

Glass Hydrometer

This is a device floated in a sample of beer or wort to measure the specific gravity of your brew. You'll need to cool whatever sample you use to room temperature. The glass hydrometer is a dependable piece of equipment, but it has downsides.

First of all, it requires a fairly large sample of liquid in order to take a reading, and since that liquid can't go back in the fermenter, it's never going to be beer. Another problem is that the actual numbers are printed on a paper insert inside the hydrometer. That paper can shift, causing inaccurate readings. Finally, the hydrometer is made of glass. It's practically a home brewer's rite of passage to break your first one at a crucial moment.

Hydrometer

Refractometer

This is more expensive than a hydrometer but will avoid the latter's limitations. A refractometer can cost up to $50. It's worth buying one with automatic temperature compensation.

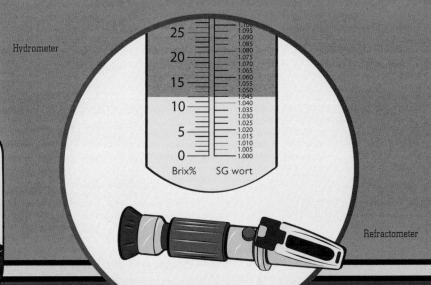

Refractometer

Not only does the refractometer involve a much smaller sample of wort to get an accurate reading, but you won't have to wait for that sample to cool down. The refractometer is great during the brew day as you can take quick readings during your sparge, before and after your boil. The only problem is that readings are skewed once fermentation starts and alcohol is being created. This can be overcome with the use of an online calculator, which will be able to factor the alcohol into the equation. The hassle factor is a small price to pay for getting to make beer and pretend that you're looking through a telescope at the same time.

Here is what it looks like when you look through the lens (the blue line is dependent on the concentration of sugars in your wort sample). The twelve level is a typical starting gravity.

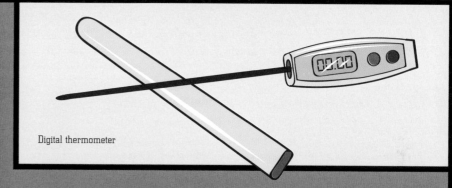
Digital thermometer

Thermometer

This has some of the same problems as the hydrometer. What may seem like being "close enough" to the correct temperature to pitch your yeast might actually be inaccurate enough to ruin your beer. Also, it's a glass tube filled with mercury. If it breaks while you're using it to measure the temperature of your beer, you have to throw that batch out. If you stick with a thermometer, buy a digital one. Not only will the digital face be easier to read than a traditional thermometer, but the time that it takes to get a reading is also usually less than eight seconds. If you're trying to measure precisely, this kind of immediate feedback is invaluable.

Digital Scale

Precision is important here. You'll be using it to measure out grain for your mash, and to measure very small amounts of hops.

Bottling Equipment

Jet Bottle Washer

This is a bent piece of metal that attaches to a utility sink (although you can buy adaptors for the kitchen sink) and blasts a stream of water into bottles, carboys, and hoses. It really cuts down on the amount of time that it will take to rinse and clean your bottles.

Bottle Brush

Look for one with sturdy bristles and a slightly flexible handle. A bottle brush isn't always required if you're in the habit of rinsing your bottles as you drink them.

Bottle Tree

A standard one will hold about twenty-four bottles and will allow your bottles to drain and dry. The deluxe models come with a bottle rinser that mounts to the top of the tree. These shoot a stream of sanitizer into the bottles when you press the bottle down onto them.

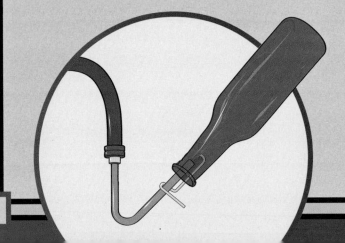

Star San is our favorite brand of sanitizer. It's an odorless and flavorless acid-based, no-rinse solution (when mixed at the right concentration). It works effectively within one to two minutes of contact time. Be sure to read the label and follow the instructions in order to get the proportion of the mix right.

Racking Cane

In order to get the beer into the bottles once they're clean, you'll need a racking cane that attaches to a piece of tubing. You also need a shutoff clamp for the tubing, which will allow you to stop the flow of beer to the bottles. This assembly will enable you to siphon your beer into bottles. To get the siphon going (don't use your mouth), fill the hose with water or sanitizer up to the elbow of the racking cane. Ensure the destination for your beer is below the source of the beer for a gravity flow.

Drain the water/sanitizer in the tube into a separate container, at which point the beer will be siphoned up behind it. Use the shutoff clamp on the hose to stop the flow once the beer starts to come out, and then transfer the hose to your bottles. Use the shutoff clamp as necessary to stop the flow of beer to the bottles as you fill them. Sometimes your hands will be slippery, and you don't want to waste any beer as you're fumbling for a bottle.

Swingtop Bottles

You can buy these at a home brew store. Using swingtop bottles means you'll never have to buy a bottle capper. All you have to do is make sure the gaskets are sterile before you bottle. If you don't want to shell out a lot of money, you can find a bar near your house that sells Grolsch and attempt to make a deal with the bar manager. After all, to the bar, they're only worth the deposit after they're empty.

Bottle Capper

If you decide that you want to use standard 12-ounce bottles, you're going to need a bottle capper. Make sure that your bottle necks aren't threaded for a screw-top cap. That will lead to an improper seal, which will allow carbonation to leech out of your home brew, and potentially let contaminants in.

There are two standard styles of bottle cappers. The first is a handheld model which has a central space for the bottle crown cap and two levers on the sides to seal the cap onto the bottle. The second variety is a bench capper. This has a single lever that pushes the crown down on to the bottle, sealing it.

Chillers

The final stage before pitching your yeast is chilling the wort to a more yeast-friendly temperature. For the 1-gal. (4 L) brewer, this can be done by using a simple ice bath. Fill your kitchen sink with ice and water, and set the pot in it. Although this method takes longer, it has the benefit of being cheap and simple.

For the 5-gal. (19 L) brewer, an ice bath will take an exceedingly long time to cool the wort. Herein lies another opportunity to put your handiwork to the test and create either an immersion chiller or a counterflow chiller.

Immersion Chiller

This is usually a copper coil immersed into the boiling wort within the last five minutes of the boil, which acts to sanitize it. The immersion chiller is then hooked up to a cold water source and the water flows through the coils in the pot and back out to the drain. The immersion chiller is simple to operate and is relatively simple to make using a 25–50-ft. (7½–15-m) long copper coil purchased at your local hardware store. Cooling should take fifteen to thirty minutes.

Counterflow Chiller

This is a bit harder to make, but will cool your wort faster and allows for the use of a hop back. The counterflow chiller is a pipe within a garden hose (make sure the hose is rubber, as the water gets hot). The inner pipe contains your hot wort, while the outer hose has cold water running through it. The two liquids run in opposite directions, resulting in cooled wort and hot water.

A 25-ft. (7^1/$_2$-m) copper coil normally allows for sufficient wort contact time. We've dialed in our counterflow chiller to where ground water enters at 50°F (10°C) and exits at 104°F (40°C), while reducing the wort from 212°F (100°C) to 64°F (18°C) in under twenty minutes. Sanitize both pipes thoroughly before use.

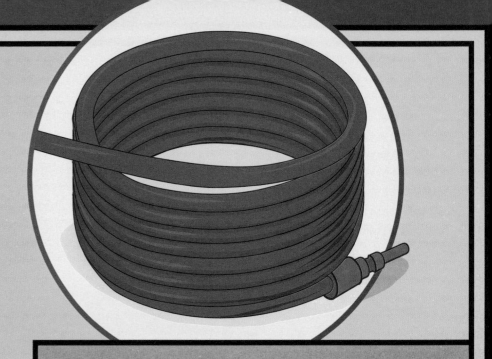

Make Your Own

There are lots of instructions online which detail how to make both an immersion and counterflow chiller. If you don't have time for DIY, you can purchase one from your local home brew store—but make sure you find an immersion chiller that matches the dimensions of your brew kettle.

Grain Mills

Milling your own grain is simply unnecessary when you can have it milled at your home brew store for a minimal charge. Grain mills are typically in the $100+ range, and become even more expensive when you consider the hopper you'll need to feed the grain into the rollers.

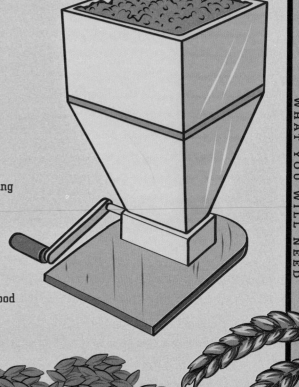

Grain lasts longest in a cool, dry space and in order for a grain mill to be more cost effective than buying milled stuff, you would need to buy sacks at a time. By the time you're using that much grain, you're going to be in a better position to evaluate your need for a mill.

If you do get to the point where you want to mill your own grain, remember that the objective is to simply crack the grain open, exposing the starch inside while keeping the husk undamaged. This will require optimization of the mill settings. The amount of space between the rollers may not seem like an obstacle to making good beer, but it's an important variable to consider.

Chapter

2

The Brewing Process

Right, you've got your ingredients and equipment and you've decided on a recipe: now it's time to roll up your sleeves and, literally, get cooking. By following the instructions contained in this chapter, you'll take your first steps into the world of brewing. In just under two weeks from now, you will be drinking your own beer.

First Things First

To start, we'd like to emphasize a note of caution. Most brewers would agree that the following single rule is the most important one in the business: hygiene.

All equipment and all your working surfaces should be sterilized clean, because if any dirt or microscopic bug creeps into the process, your efforts could be doomed. We don't want to scare you off, just underline how important cleanliness is in brewing.

You just need to make sure you've purchased a safe proprietary sterilizing liquid. Star San is a good food-safe sanitizer—or a similar product, which a parent would be happy using to clean a baby's milk bottle.

Take Note . . .

Another important tool at the start of the brewing process is a notebook. You'll find it useful to have information about all parts of the process, so that if something goes wrong you'll be able to fix it next time. If your hop addition was late, you'll want to know. If your water at mash in was a little too hot, you'll want to remember that for next time. Think of your notes as being like a black box on an airplane.

Preparing and Heating Your Water

Depending on the method you've chosen for treating your water (see page 10), you might need to plan ahead a little. If you're using bottled water, there's less effort required—all you need to do is to add a small amount of gypsum to make it brew ready.

If you've decided to use tap water, either boil it first or add Campden tablets to remove any chlorine. The boiling option can be time consuming, whereas Campden tablets simplify the process, and eliminate boiling. One tablet will treat about 20 gallons (76 L) of water, so you will probably need only half a tablet.

If you're new to all-grain brewing, you'll be surprised by how much water you will need for brewing. Unlike extract brewing—where you really only need the amount suggested on the can—all-grain brewing has additional processes that also involve water. This is partly because the grain soaks up a lot of liquid during the mashing process. For a 5-gallon (19 L) batch of beer, you're probably going to need to prepare double that amount of water.

Because the starches in your grain only convert into sugars at a certain temperature, you need to heat the water to a specific temperature, which will be somewhere above your mash temperature. After all, your grain is at room temperature, and it will cause your brewing liquor to cool down quickly. If you're aiming to mash in at 152°F (67°C), you will probably want your brewing liquor to be around 165°F (74°C) before you add it to the grain.

Weighing and Milling Your Grain

Make sure the quantities of grain for your chosen recipe are correct. Your local brewing supply store should be able to grind your grain to order, then all you have to do is measure out the amounts you need. Easy! (Remember to allow for the weight of the receptacle you're using to hold the grain.)

If you're milling your own grain, it's important to get the consistency right. If the grain is too big, you're not going to get the kind of starch conversion you want. If it's too small, it's going to be powdery, which will make it harder to lauter properly (don't worry, we'll explain what this means very shortly). You need to break the grain into two or three pieces, so to get the consistency right you might need to adjust the width between the grain mill rollers. Don't be afraid to play around with the settings on the mill.

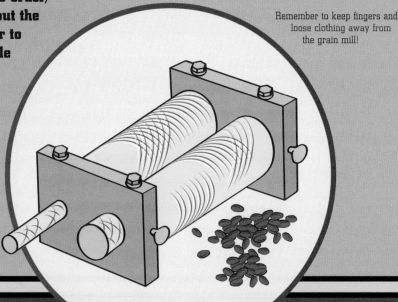

Remember to keep fingers and loose clothing away from the grain mill!

Doughing-In for the Mash

With your water heated to the right temperature and the grain milled and measured out, it's time to mash in—adding the grain to the water in your mash tun. It's important to remember that this process begins the conversion of grain starches into sugars.

In order to get the enzymes in the grain to do that, you need to keep an eye on two things: the temperature of the mash has to be right, and you must avoid clumping—more on that in a moment.

Add grain to the mash in a steady stream. Do not simply dump the grain in the mash in one dollop.

First, different styles of beers require different enzymes to be working to convert the starch into sugar. Recipes aiming for simple sugars tend to require mashing at around 152°F (67°C), while recipes aiming to contain more complex sugars in the beer need to mash in at around 160°F (71°C).

One or two degrees difference in your mash temperature is unlikely to matter very much. However, more than that will make all the difference between highly fermentable sugars, which create the alcohol, and residual sugars, which will create mouth-feel and character.

Keep an eye on the temperature with a digital thermometer, and you shouldn't have a lot of trouble getting it right.

Clumping

Now to avoid clumping: the size of your milled grain is important because of its interaction with the brewing water. If your milled grain clumps together, it can change the efficiency of that interaction and prevent it from converting properly—and that could mean weak beer! So, it's important to keep stirring until the consistency is even—hence the mash paddle.

The mash will take between half an hour and one hour. It depends on the grain you're using. It's usually best to err on the side of caution and give the mash a full hour. When you think the process is complete, what you've got is no longer water. It's wort, and it now needs to be separated from the "spent" grain.

Stir as the grain is added to the water. Continue to stir until all the grain has been thoroughly mixed in with the water.

Vorlauf, Lautering, and Sparging

Three technical terms—two of them from the great brewing nation, Germany—but don't be intimidated by the words. They're just part of the process we're going through, and here's what they mean.

Vorlauf

In German it literally means to "go ahead." In brewing terms, it means clarifying the hazy wort from the spent grains—drawing off the liquid from the solids and slowly recycling it back into the mash tun over the grains which are settling firmly in the bottom. You need a pitcher in which to collect the drawn-off wort. This is called the "first runnings."

Lautering

This is a process to squeeze all the remaining sugars from the grain in the bottom of the mash tun, known by the German name *lautering*. The grain "bed" has been settled by vorlaufing. First, open the valve on your mash tun and allow the wort to run into the brew kettle. Next, you're going to pour fresh water slowly over the grain bed.

Advanced Techniques

While vorlaufing can be done with just a pitcher and a delicate touch, pouring the wort through a wide-bottomed colander will help you distribute the first runnings evenly over the top of the grain bed. The holes in the colander will ensure that the wort is distributed gently and evenly over the surface of the grain. This can also be used for the sparging water.

Sparging

Remember how we said you would need about 10 gallons (38 L) of heated water for all-grain brewing? This is where the rest of that water comes in. This is the sparging water. Heat this to about 170°F (77°C). Any hotter, and you risk leaching harsh-tasting tannins out of the grain. Pour the sparging water slowly and gently over the grain in the bottom of the tun, about a pitcher at a time. Distribute it evenly over the top of the grain bed without disturbing the grains too much. Ideally, keep the level of liquid just above the height of the grain bed, while slowly drawing off this sparging water until you have about 6 gallons (23 L) of wort collected in the brew kettle. Here's the process, from vorlaufing to sparging:

1 Use a pitcher to collect the first runnings from your mash tun. Open the valve only slightly to regulate flow.

2 Distribute the first runnings over the top of the grain bed, using a gentle pouring action so as not to disturb the bed.

3 As the wort leaves the grain bed on its way to the brew kettle, the level of liquid in the mash falls, displaying the top of the grain bed.

3

4

4 At this point, slightly hotter water is introduced in order to sparge, or rinse, the residual sugars from the grain.

5 All of this wort will flow from the mash tun (here, shown elevated) into the brew kettle, represented here as a keggle.

5

Check, Bring to the Boil, and Measure

With the wort collected, you need to take a sample and measure the specific gravity, using either a hydrometer or a refractometer. This tells you how much sugar is in your wort, and it gives you an idea of how efficient the conversion that took place in your mash tun was. Because you've collected 6 gallons (23 L) of wort, the reading may be slightly lower than your recipe says it should be, but don't worry. You are now going to boil the wort for an hour so there will be a lot of evaporation. As some of the water content boils off, the sugars become more concentrated in the liquid and the gravity of the wort will increase.

Add a small sample of wort to the face of the refractometer using a pipette to determine the gravity of the wort.

While your wort is bubbling, this is a good opportunity to measure out the hops. As you might need to add hops several times, it's probably worthwhile measuring them out into separate sterilized plastic or glass containers.

Measuring hops is a more delicate procedure than measuring out grains because you're dealing with much smaller quantities. You're also dealing with hop pellets, which are concentrated and so look very small and insignificant. You might think the amount looks small, but it's best to follow the recipe strictly rather than thinking another handful might be OK. If you do add extra, be sure to note this in your brew log. You'll want to know how it changed the finished beer.

Leaf Hops

When measuring leaf hops, as opposed to pellets, you may need a bigger container to sit on top of the scale. Leaf hops are much lighter, take up more room, and are nowhere near as compact as pellets.

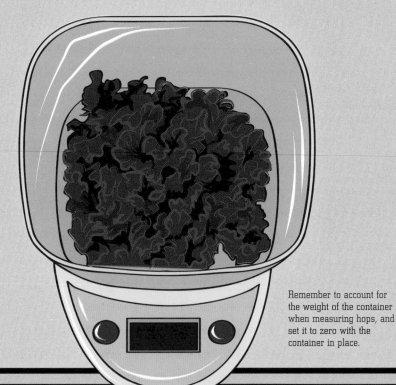

Remember to account for the weight of the container when measuring hops, and set it to zero with the container in place.

Hop Additions

Your first hop addition will be the bittering hop portion of your recipe, and you need to add it as soon as your wort comes to a rolling boil in the kettle. There's no reason to stir the hops into the wort at this stage. They will mix easily enough in the swirling brew on their own.

You need to pay fairly close attention to the time in order to make sure you add flavor and aroma hops at the right moment during your hour-long boil. A cell phone alarm is ideal.

Stay close to the brew kettle after each hop addition because the alpha acids in the hops can cause the height of the boil to increase dramatically. After the level decreases, scrape any hops on the side of the kettle back down into the wort in order to ensure they're used.

When you've finished boiling and removed the wort from the heat, the next process is whirlpooling. No matter how good a job you did creating a grain bed in the mash tun, there will be some residual pieces of grain in the brew kettle. And there'll be hop vegetable matter that you don't want in your fermenter.

When adding hops to the boil, you don't need to stir. The boil will do the work for you.

"Whirlpooling" means stirring your wort with a long-handled plastic or metal spoon which has been sterilized. Best not to use wood, which is more prone to being contaminated. Stir in one direction around the outside edge of the brew kettle. This creates a centrifugal force that drags down any solid material to the middle of the bottom of the kettle. Give it five minutes, and then let it rest for ten. Einstein discovered this phenomenon while stirring his tea!

When brewing a hoppy beer, the hops will collect in the center of the whirlpool and deposit at the bottom of the kettle.

Whirlpooling

You do not need to create a maelstrom in order to make the whirlpool work. As long as the motion is in the same direction, and there's a visible downward draft in the center of the kettle, you are doing it right.

Cooling Off

Immersion chiller

Everything up to this point has been made sterile by boiling the wort. Now that it has finished boiling, you want to avoid anything that is not absolutely sterile coming into contact with it, because it could introduce bacteria into your wort. Therefore, it's important to work through this stage as quickly as possible.

If you have a wort chiller, all you have to do is run the wort through the tubing of the chiller while the chiller itself is submerged in ice water. From there you can run it directly into the fermenter. This is ideal because you're cooling a small portion of the wort at once.

If you don't have a chiller, you'll have to place the brew kettle in an ice bath. This will

certainly take longer, but as long as you don't remove the lid from the kettle during the process, bacteria should be kept at bay.

The length of time for the cooling process depends on which cooling method you adopt, and how effective it is. You must get the wort down to about 68°F (20°C). Keep checking with a thermometer.

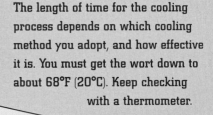

Stir the water around the kettle to allow cold water to get at the metal surface.

The Fermenting Stage

If you're using a plastic pail as a fermenter, it may seem logical simply to tip the contents of the kettle into the pail. Don't do this. Remember, we've gone to the trouble of stirring the wort to settle the trub to the bottom of the kettle. You don't want to agitate that stuff if you can help it.

You should siphon the wort into the fermenter with the help of a long plastic tube (sterilized, of course). If your fermenter is positioned lower than the kettle, gravity will do the work for you. If you have a kettle with a ball valve at the bottom, you don't even have to siphon, you just open it and the liquid will flow through the tube to the fermenter.

Using a Pail

If you're using a pail to ferment in, you may be able to skip the tubing altogether. Since the trub is already at the bottom of the kettle, it's possible, with good care, to pour the wort directly into the pail. Pour slowly and gently, to disturb as little of the trub as possible. The action will have the added benefit of aerating your wort.

If the kettle is positioned above the fermenter, on a countertop, for instance . . .

. . . it will make it easier to siphon your wort through the tubing into your fermenter.

Pitching Your Yeast

Before adding yeast to begin fermentation, you should take a reading of the specific gravity of the wort. This will tell you the original gravity—how much sugar the yeast has to ferment—and enable you to calculate the amount of alcohol in your finished beer. If you used a hydrometer, it's best from a hygiene perspective not to put the sample back into the fermenter.

Also, once the wort has reached the desired temperature, you should oxygenate it. In home-brewing terms, this means shaking the fermenter for a couple of minutes. Alternately, you can splash the wort during the transfer to the fermenter in order to oxygenate it.

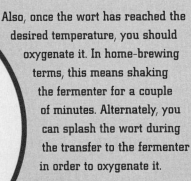

Adding the Yeast

When the wort has cooled to between 65 and 70°F (18 and 21°C), it's time to add the yeast. Whether you are using wet or dry yeast, it's as simple as opening the packet and following instructions.

Placing Your Airlock

Once the lid of the fermenter is in place, place your airlock in the hole at the center of the lid. The airlock prevents any airborne contaminants from getting at your beer while letting carbon dioxide out. You should fill the airlock with a mixture of sterile water and sanitizer. Alternately, you could use a blow-off tube that will channel the carbon dioxide into a bucket of sterile water and sanitizer.

Here we see a standard airlock filled with sanitizer, attached to a pail fermenter.

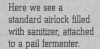

And here is a makeshift blow-off tube that uses a jar of sanitizer.

Fermentation

Ideally, you should place your fermenter in an out-of-the way shaded spot with a constant temperature. A steady temperature is important for making sure that you will get the flavor you want out of your yeast.

If your fermenter is standing in direct sunlight, there's always a chance that the light will raise the temperature. We recommend a closet or the corner of a basement.

If this is your first-time experience of brewing at home, the temptation to open the fermenter and check on the progress of your beer can be overwhelming. Don't! You've gone to a lot of trouble to make sure that your beer isn't infected, so opening the fermenter to take a peek is a good way to ruin all that work.

Leave it Alone!

Your airlock will start to bubble somewhere between four and seventy-two hours after pitching the yeast. You might want to check on the bubbling once a day during the first seventy-two hours, just to make sure the yeast is at work.

It will take about a week for your wort to turn into proper beer. It's still not ready though. There'll be a lot of stuff in it you still want to get rid of, such as leftover bits of hops and grain, and blobs of dead yeast.

If you leave your beer in a closet, you won't be quite so tempted to peek inside the fermenter.

It's for this reason that racking, or siphoning, the green beer from your fermenter into another container, such as a carboy, is a good idea, so as to remove as much undesirable material as possible before bottling. To rack your beer, you need a sterilized piece of clear plastic hose attached to a rigid clear plastic tube. The tube goes to the bottom of the fermenter and the tubing goes to the carboy. Transferring the beer from one receptacle to the other will get rid of the majority of the

When racking, you should place the original fermenter on a countertop in order to make siphoning your beer easier.

Spent Yeast

After racking, there's still quite a bit of live yeast in your beer. By moving your beer to a different vessel, you're leaving behind the dead yeast cells that have already done their work.

detritus at the bottom of your fermenter. Your beer will probably still not be completely clear. There will still be little floating bits of yeast. This may look a little unsavory, but it's fine at this stage.

Leave your racked beer in a dark place. Light, especially modern fluorescent energy saving bulbs, can create unwanted, skunky flavors. Leave it alone for between three and seven days.

Preparing to Bottle

After the racked period, it'll be time to check if your beer is ready to bottle. Draw a sample and read the specific gravity, using either a hydrometer or refractometer. You will probably get a reading much lower than the one you took when you put the wort into the fermenter. That's because the yeast has devoured the sugar content, turning it into alcohol and carbon dioxide.

At this point, a decision has to be made. If your beer has reached the final gravity listed in the recipe, it's probably ready to be bottled. If it hasn't reached the final gravity you want, you should wait a few days more for the yeast to finally finish working.

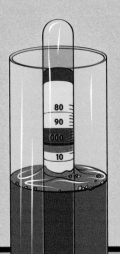

A hydrometer takes a reading of the gravity of the beer. The reading here says it is not quite finished.

Cleanliness

Make sure you have scrubbed your bottles inside and out. Any dirt on the inside of a bottle, no matter how tiny, is a potential contaminant.

The wire bottle brush is flexible, so you don't have to worry about being too gentle.

Beer Bottle Choice

Bottling is time consuming. Many people prefer swing-top bottles, such as those the Dutch Grolsch brewery uses. If you opt for 12-ounce bottles that require capping, just be sure that you're using ones that don't have twist-off tops—the threading will make it difficult, if not impossible, to use bottle caps properly.

The slightly rounded caps on normal 12-ounce bottles allow the seal of the crown to cap the bottle. Remember that the wire cage on the swing-top bottle comes with a stopper. If you are using bottles that have previously held beer, it's a good idea to replace the red gasket on the stopper. The gaskets can be picked up at your local home brew supply store, and are cheap enough to be replaced every time you bottle. After all, there might be traces of contaminants between the stopper and the gasket. If you're brewing at home to save money, the few extra cents that go into ensuring you don't contaminate your beer during bottling are not a good place to cut corners. Better safe than sorry.

Stopper

Gasket

How to Carbonate Your Beer

To ensure a good beer head, you need to add some sugar so it will carbonate in the bottle. There are a number of ways to do this.

The first is to place sugar directly into the bottles. While this will certainly do the job, it requires some attention to detail. For a 12-ounce bottle, you need to add approximately one teaspoonful of sugar to the bottle prior to putting any beer into it. There are some drawbacks to this method. The sugar may not fully dissolve, leaving a sludgy

residue that you really don't want in your finished beer. Also, each teaspoon measurement needs to be precisely the same amount for each bottle. Adding too much sugar can lead to over carbonation, which can lead to bottles exploding in your fridge.

Carbonation tablets take all of the guesswork out of these measurements—you simply drop a different number of them into each 12-ounce bottle, based on the desired level of carbonation. This might seem like an ideal solution, but the drawback nonetheless remains as to whether or not the tablets will dissolve properly. If they do not dissolve, you may end up with floating chalk-like bits of sugar in your finished beer. This is undesirable.

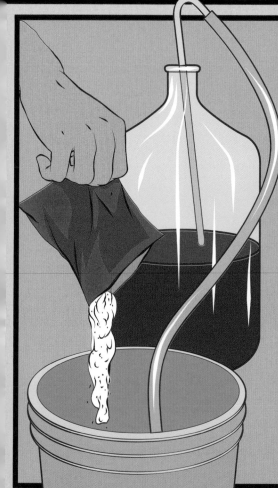

The best option is to add priming sugar directly to the beer before you put it into bottles. You don't have to think of carbonating on a per-bottle level, as this method embraces the entire batch of beer. Dissolve two-thirds of a cup (85 g) of sugar in two cups (450 ml) of water. Bring to a boil, and then quickly cool it down. Once the mixture is cooled, stir it into your beer. In addition to being slightly faster than putting the sugar into individual bottles, it means the beer will be less prone to infection since the sugar solution will have been made sterile through boiling.

If you add the sugar without dissolving it first in water, be sure to stir as you pour it in.

Bottle Bomb

Picture this: you're sitting in your living room, watching the game on TV, and you suddenly hear a loud bang from wherever you're storing your bottles. You run to the closet or fridge and find a puddle of foaming beer and shards of glass. This is the result of over-carbonated beer, and it's something that will probably happen at least once during your home brewing career. Since there's no completely foolproof way to avoid this, it's best not to leave carbonating bottles in a carpeted area, which is certain to end up smelling like beer for at least a month after a big boom.

Bottling

Bottling is preferably a two-person job. Using a sterile length of tube to get your beer to flow into a number of bottles can be logistically difficult by yourself. Ideally, you want to cap each bottle as it fills.

This may be a good opportunity to enlist the help of your friends. After all, there is the promise of beer at the end of the process. Usually this will be enough to make even the most work-shy of your acquaintances offer their eager assistance.

However, if you do find yourself working alone, some home brew kits now come with a clamp, which will stop the flow of beer through the tube without putting a brake on the siphoning action. This gives you the luxury of filling as many bottles as you want at one time, which can be invaluable in a small workspace. There's nothing worse than realizing you've run out of space and the flow of beer isn't stopping.

The clamp "pinches" the tubing and thereby stops you from wasting any beer.

Bottle Caps

Bottle caps must be sterile. Give them a rinse in a sanitizing solution before you cap. If you find that any caps have rusty discoloration, you should throw them out. If a cap seems not to have sealed completely, simply remove the cap and use a new one. For this reason, it's probably best to have extra bottle caps lying around.

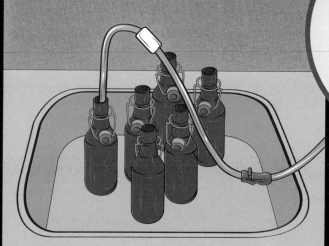

The Grand Opening!

Your beer will take about a week to carbonate. But don't think you're helping things along by putting the beer into the fridge. To carbonate correctly, you should keep your beer at room temperature.

Open one bottle to check on its effervescence. If it's frothy enough, you are in business! If it's a bit flat, you might want to leave the other bottles a little while longer. On the other hand, it'll probably taste good enough anyway!

Before caps go on bottles, they're properly referred to as crowns. They're only "caps" once they've been used.

Chapter 3

The Easy Brew Method

For a gentle introduction to the art of home brewing—and if you don't quite feel ready for the all-grain recipes featured later in these pages—you're in for a nice surprise: you can go the "Easy Brew" route. This involves brewing with malt extract; and, trust us, there's absolutely nothing wrong with malt extract if you're a home brewer.

Malt Extract Brewing

As a beginner, it might be worthwhile brewing with malt extract first. There's nothing wrong with malt extract: it's a simpler way into the art of brewing, it can save you time, and the final product can be good.

Malt extract is a concentrated version of the wort that results from mashing with grain. It allows you to skip the mash portion of the brewing process by replacing it with extract, and the entire session can take as little as two hours. But it also means that you sacrifice some control over the final flavor of your beer.

This chapter explains the advantages and disadvantages of using malt extract, and points you in the direction of the most flavorsome options. The method that we have chosen cheats slightly by entirely avoiding the use of a mash tun. It is very effective, and hopefully it will help you to develop an instinct for some of the properties of specialty grains, which you will be using in the other recipes in the book. In brewing, instinct is important.

Basic varieties of malt extract, delineated by their color.

Styles of Extract

The quality of extract available these days means that you can choose one that's suitable for a specific style of beer. You can purchase extract made from wheat or pilsner malt, for example. If you have friends who are gluten intolerant, you can even make beer out of Sorghum extract in order to be able to serve them your beer.

It will depend on the quality of the home brew supply near you whether or not you can obtain a "designer" malt extract. What you will probably discover is that there are extract kits that are designed to allow you to brew specific styles of beer without a great deal of effort. In these cases, the extract is usually pre-hopped, meaning that you will only have to add water to the malt extract of your choice and boil in order to make beer.

Brewing supply companies make a variety of these malt extract products. While they're worth trying as an initial step as a home brewer, it's worth remembering that the end results might not be to your taste, simply because they have been designed by someone else whose taste will differ from yours.

Liquid Malt Extract

Liquid Malt Extract can be hard to measure accurately, which is why it comes in preset amounts.

Dry Malt Extract

Dry Malt Extract can become sticky very quickly. Make sure anything that it comes in contact with is dry.

Style and Profile

American Pale Ale has become the mainstay of the craft brewing scene, not only in North America, but also in England where it has caught on in a big way over the last decade. This comes as no surprise since it owes part of its heritage to Extra Special Bitters, which have long been a mainstay of British brewing. Although there are many versions of it to choose from, the one with the longest heritage is Sierra Nevada Pale Ale, which is as close to being the originator of the style as it is possible to be. In all probability, if you're a big enough beer fan to be reading this book, you'll have tried it a few times. Our recipe falls square in the middle of the style guidelines.

BJCP Vital Statistics for American Pale Ale

American Pale Ale can range from subtle hopping to pronounced hopping, sometimes intruding on the India Pale Ale category. The color can range from gold to deep copper. Typically, West Coast hops are used, but some varieties use English or German ones.

OG: 1.045–1.060	**BJCP** = Beer Judge Certification Program	
IBUs: 30–45	**FG:** 1.010–1.015	
SRM: 5–14	**ABV:** 4.5–6.2%	

Partial Mash Brewing

Fortunately, it's possible to brew with extract and give the finished beer the Pale Ale character that you want thanks to a process called Partial Mash Brewing. It's not a great deal more complicated than adding malt extract to boiling water, but there will be additional steps. If you follow our instructions, you'll be on your way to a tasty Pale Ale in practically no time.

The recipe we recommend in this chapter requires little in the way of additional ingredients, but allows you to customize your beer in the same way that all grain brewing does. In terms of recipe design, what you probably want to do is start with the lightest malt extract you can find and add color and character with specialty grains. While it will probably be some time before you feel comfortable designing your own recipes, this advice is applicable to any style you might choose to brew using this method.

As the color of the grain gets darker, so does the beer you make with it.

Partial Mash Pale Ale

Extract American Pale Ale

Malt

LBs	OZ	KG	MALT TYPE
6	6	2.89	Briess Gold Unhopped LME
0	8	0.227	Vienna Malt
0	8	0.227	Crystal/Caramel 15

	SPECIFIC GRAVITY	PLATO
Original Gravity	1.051	12.6
Final Gravity	1.013	3.3
Yeast Attenuation	74%	
Color	6	
Batch Size	5 Gallons (just under 19 L)	
Mash Efficiency	75%	

Hops

USE	TIME	OZ	GRAMS	VARIETY	AA
Boil	60 mins	2	57	Cascade	5.5%
Boil	5 mins	1	28½	Cascade	5.5%

Boil for 60 minutes.

Cool and ferment at 62–68°F (17–20°C) with Wyeast 1056 American Ale.

IBUs	40.5
ABV	5.10%
ABW	4.00%

The Process

The brewing process is fairly straightforward. Fill whichever pot you're using as a brew kettle with just under the amount of water you need for a batch of 5 gallons (19 L) and get ready to bring it to the boil. It's important to remember that you will be adding liquid to your kettle, and that it will count toward the total volume of beer that you're making.

Since we're using liquid malt extract in this recipe, you need to understand something about the nature of the product. It's incredibly viscous and sticky at room temperature, so if you can find a way of heating the container slightly—for example, by partially submerging it in warm water—it will help you later. For safety's sake, it's important not to let the liquid malt extract become too hot. It is a sugary syrup, and you should take care not to get any hot liquid malt extract on your skin.

Choosing a Grain Bag

You will need some kind of bag to hold the grain. You can purchase grain bags specifically for this purpose. Some of the bags are simply muslin or cotton pouches with drawstrings that you can cinch closed. The benefit of these pouches is that they will stand up to repeated use.

The better option is the muslin sheath, which has no drawstring and can simply be tied off with twine or be knotted. Their only downside is that they can be quite fragile. One option home brewers have tried with success is one leg of a pair of panty hose. If you're a man and the salesperson gives you a strange look, you may as well explain it's only for beer, and the look will be even stranger.

The pouch-style grain bag, with its drawstring, comes in various sizes.

But thankfully, so do panty hose.

Before running the cans under the tap, check that they are not open. That's a good way to lose your malt extract.

Steeping Your Grain

Instead of creating an actual mash you would have to filter, it's easier to steep your grain in the water as it comes up to temperature. The results are practically the same and it saves a significant amount of time.

1 With your pot of water on the stove, begin to heat it up, and take the temperature periodically until it reaches approximately 120°F (49°C). Because it is a large quantity of water, you will be able to complete step two while this is happening.

2 Insert your grain into whichever style of grain bag you have chosen. If the opening is wide enough, you should be able to pour it in slowly, distributing it by gently shaking the bag. You may want to use a piece of wire to keep the top of the bag stretched open.

3 Make sure that the top of the bag is completely closed and submerge the grains in the water once it reaches the desired temperature. If possible, suspend it so that it doesn't touch the bottom and burn the material of the bag.

2

3

1

4 The water that you're working with will heat up slowly, extracting some of the fermentable material from these specialty grains. As the temperature of the water rises above 160°F (71°C), you should remove the bag with the grains so that you don't extract any bitterness from them.

Diastatic Power

The specialty grains that we're using in this recipe will impart color, but they will not contribute all of the fermentable material that they would if they were being used in a regular mash. Specialty grains are modified in such a way that they are unable to convert in a mash by themselves. The enzymatic power of a malt is called "diastatic power," and specialty grains possess fewer of these enzymes than pale malts, which undergo less modification in the malting process.

5 When removing the grain bag from your kettle, it's important to remember that the contents of the bag are very hot and that the grains are now wet. It will be heavier than it was when you submerged it. It is a good idea to have a strainer or colander on hand to place the bag in, since it will be uncomfortably hot to the touch.

Adding the Malt

As the water comes to a boil, add your (now hopefully runny) liquid malt extract. Add it in a steady stream and stir as vigorously as you can without spilling liquid over the sides of the kettle. If the extract settles at the bottom of the kettle near the element or flame, it will have a tendency to scorch because it is very thick and full of sugars.

You really don't want that to happen as it will create problems with the flavor of your beer. What you're trying to do is get the liquid malt extract to dilute into the now grain-flavored water. Once you've done that, you've made wort without using a mash tun.

There will be a significant amount of hot steam coming off the water, and malt extract pours slowly. You may choose to use a protective glove.

Different Malt Extracts

We recommend using a basic light malt extract for your beer, and this is for good reason. When you're looking at cans labeled "dark," it's hard to say exactly which malts have made it dark. You want to control the flavor as much as possible, and light extract will allow you that much more control.

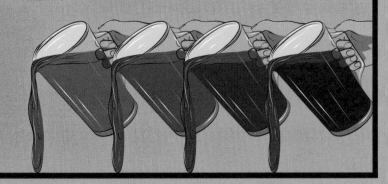

Hopping

The hopping schedule for this recipe is simple; it's a single hop pale ale. All of the hops involved are Cascade. You're going to need 2 oz. (57 g) as a bittering addition at the start of the boil, and a single ounce (28 g) five minutes from the end of the boil.

One important thing to realize is that because you have used hops in this recipe, there will still be sediment in your wort once it has finished boiling. Liquid malt extract, even if it is very well made, may also contain some sediment. For these reasons, you will still have to whirlpool your pale ale wort after it has finished boiling.

The process of cooling the wort after the boil is discussed elsewhere in this book, as is the addition of yeast. Beyond the actual brewing process, making beer with extract is not significantly different from brewing with grain. Hopefully, this experience will inspire you to try a full malt brew when your malt extract beer supply begins to run low.

In the meantime, you can always continue to research the different varieties of American Pale Ale that are available. The good news is that there are literally thousands of them on offer, since the style is almost universal among craft brewers.

You may want to research what you're drinking, and take notes on which combinations of hops you enjoy. There's no reason you can't adapt the recipe to your taste.

It's always a good idea to measure out your hops well in advance of when you will need them.

Chapter 4

Belgian Wit

Belgian Witbier is a light and refreshing beer that has become a staple of summer patios and backyards the world over. It's perfect for long, hot days when a cooling drink is what's required. Working a Belgian Witbier into your brewing repertoire will keep invitations to friends' and neighbors' barbecues rolling in for years to come.

A European Tradition

Belgian Witbier is a style with a long history, dating back to the medieval period in Europe. The style colorfully illustrates how brewing was influenced by the ingredients at hand at the time—in this case, wheat, coriander seed, and orange peel.

The coriander seed and orange peel are present for two reasons. Witbier descends from a beverage called Gruit, in which brewers used ingredients other than hops to impart flavor and bitterness to their beer.

Citrus-and-coriander is a flavor combination used the world over.

These ingredient-led types of experimentation were possible because of what was then the Dutch Empire. (Neither cilantro nor oranges are native to Belgium, which in those distant days—the 1600s—lay under Dutch rule.) The bitter orange peel typically used is referred to as Curaçao Orange, which links it specifically to a Caribbean island colonized by the Dutch in the early seventeenth century. The expansion of trade provided by roaming Dutch, British, French, Spanish, and Portuguese seafarers brought a wide range of new spices, fruits, and other produce never before seen in Europe. With new ingredients at their disposal, brewers in

Belgium were able to modify their recipes in order to create a new range of flavors, which eventually became Witbier. Instead of using nettles or bog myrtle to make Gruit, they were able to use more exotic ingredients. At this time,

Some of the iconic Witbier glasses require two hands. This is a good thing.

hops were becoming far more widely used throughout Germany due to the Bavarian purity law of 1516 (see page 13). The alchemy of using hops, coriander seed, and orange peel resulted in a classic beer style.

. . . and a Beer Style that Rocks

For a time, Belgian Witbier ceased to exist. Once it had been a popular beverage, but support for the style dwindled over the centuries. In the mid 1950s, the last producer of beers in that style, the Tomsin brewery in Hoegaarden (a town in the Flemish region with a one thousand-year history), shut down. Fortunately for beer drinkers worldwide, the singular efforts of one enthusiast, Pierre Celis, revived the style.

Celis had lived next to, and worked at, the Tomsin brewery. He must have loved that beer, because in 1966, he quit his job as a milkman and started his own brewery, de Kluis, in a barn. His new beer, Hoegaarden, became very popular. The brewery expanded to a new production facility in 1979. Unfortunately for Celis, the brewery was destroyed by a fire in 1985, forcing a partial sale of the site to a much larger company which has since turned the former milkman's beer into a global brand.

To cut a long story short, Celis relocated to Austin, Texas, and started the Celis brewery in 1992. It produced Celis White, another Witbier, and several other styles.

Belgium is one of the world's great beer cultures and produces the majority of the excellent Trappist monastery beers.

North Sea

NETHERLANDS

Bruges

GERMANY

Tienen

Brussels

Tomsin brewery

BELGIUM

FRANCE

LUXEMBOURG

Opening a brewery is a difficult challenge at any time in your life, but Celis did this at the age of sixty-seven. Consider the amount of faith he must have had in Witbier to attempt to start over when most people are retiring.

Pierre Celis

Celis was attracted to Texas by the calcium-rich water, and also by the local wheat. This combination ensured that Celis White measured up to his high standards.

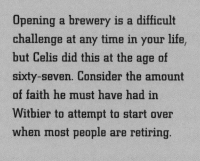

NEW MEXICO (USA)

TEXAS (USA)

Austin

MEXICO

Gulf of Mexico

Austin has always been a city for cultural pioneers. In addition to being the live music capital of the world, it boasts a large number of microbreweries.

The tell-tale sign that his belief was spot on can be seen in the fact that both Hoegaarden and Celis himself continued to win international awards long after his involvement ended. The style is now widely imitated. All of this stems from the dedication and effort of one milkman who took a risk. In doing so, he resurrected a beer style and became a role model for pioneering craft brewers across North America. It's no wonder the beer world views him as a hero.

Style and Profile

The literal translation for *Witbier* is "white beer," even though it may sound to English ears as though it might be "wheat beer." It is extremely light in color. This is due mostly to the fact that almost none of the grain ingredients for a Witbier impart a significant amount of color. In order to adhere to the style, approximately 50 percent of the grain should be wheat and the other 50 percent should be very lightly kilned barley, either a pale malt or a pilsner malt. Some of the wheat can be replaced with other grains, such as oats or millet. This also accounts for a significant amount of the haze that is apparent in the beer when it's cold.

BJCP Vital Statistics for Witbier

Witbier tends to be easy on the eyes and gentle on the palate. Hop bitterness is quite low and you'll want to use fairly mildly flavored European hops. The interest comes from the yeast character and the spice additions. Some tartness can be delicious.		
	OG: 1.044–1.052	BJCP = Beer Judge Certification Program
	IBUs: 10–20	**FG:** 1.008–1.012
	SRM: 2–4	**ABV:** 4.5–5.5%

Wheat is comparatively high in protein, which, along with the yeast, makes Witbier opaque. The real difficulty lies in getting the beer to remain light in color, and it's for this reason that it contains no specialty malt. The wheat may not impart significant color, but it does give the style a lightly creamy mouthfeel. The choice of the correct strain of yeast is important to the style, since Belgian yeast tends to impart distinct flavors that include phenols. These may show up in your finished beer as a clove-like aroma. The yeast works together with the spices that define the style. The spicing must be relatively subtle, since coriander, when overused, can become soapy. This may not be a direct problem with the flavor of the beer but rather of its reception on the drinker's palate. Some people perceive the flavor of coriander to be soap-like.

Fruity Extras

You may have seen Witbier served with a slice of lemon or orange. This constitutes beer heresy according to some serious-minded experts. However, we think that if you're going to go to the trouble of making it yourself, you can do whatever you want with it. Throw a slice of lemon, or even pineapple, on the rim of the glass if the mood strikes you.

Why Fruit?

The addition of fruit to Witbier is not a new phenomenon. In fact, the only novel thing about the way it is served in North America is that the fruit slices sit on the lip of the glass. In parts of Germany, it's considered perfectly normal to add raspberry or woodruff syrup to light wheat beers, depending on the customer's personal preference.

Witbier—The Recipe

Brevity Wit

		SPECIFIC GRAVITY	PLATO
Original Gravity		1.05	12.4
Final Gravity		1.009	2.2
Yeast Attenuation		82%	
Color		3.1 SRM, Hazy Straw	
Batch Size		5 Gallons (just under 19 L)	
Mash Efficiency		75%	

Malt

LBs	OZ	KG	MALT TYPE
5	0	2.27	American Two-Row Pale Malt
4	0	1.81	Torrified Wheat
0	8	0.227	Flaked Oats

Hops

USE	TIME	OZ	GRAMS	VARIETY	AA
Boil	60 mins	1	28½	Hallertauer	4.0%
Boil	5 mins	1	28½	Hallertauer	4.0%
Boil	5 mins	¾	21½	Coriander Seed	n/a
Boil	5 mins	¾	21½	Orange Peel, bitter	n/a

IBUs	16.7
ABV	5.30%
ABW	4.25%

17 IBU

5.3% Alcohol content

The torrifying wheat treatment is the application of heat to make each kernel pop. If you did the same thing to corn, you could watch a movie.

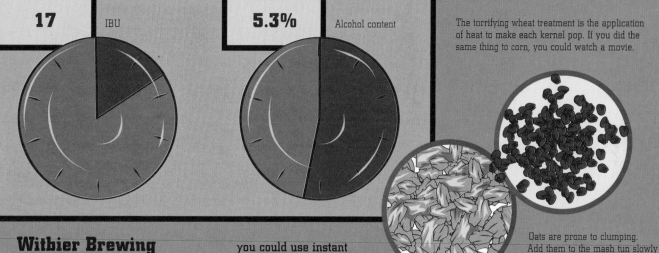

Oats are prone to clumping. Add them to the mash tun slowly to ensure even distribution.

Witbier Brewing Method

1. Mash at 150–152°F (66–67°C).
2. Boil for sixty minutes.
3. Cool and ferment at 62–75°F (17–24°C).

For our recipe, we've included oats for the mouthfeel that they impart. You can buy flaked oats from your local home brew supply store, but you could use instant oats without any detrimental effect. The reason behind the inclusion of torrified wheat is that it's a lot easier to brew with than raw wheat would be. Torrified wheat has been pre-treated to break down the cellular structure and allow for easier conversion in the mash without any pre-treatment on your part. We've gone with relatively subtle spicing, using less than an ounce (28 g) of coriander seed and bitter orange peel. Since Witbier is typically a summer beverage, you're probably going to want to enjoy more than one of them. For this reason, it's best to aim for subtlety in flavor.

Witbier Variations

If you're interested in playing around with the recipe in order to achieve a creamier mouthfeel, you can change the proportion of oats in the mash by bumping it up to as much as 15 percent. It's important to retain 50 percent pale malt because you need the enzymes from the grain in order to get an efficient conversion of starch. Therefore, you'll need to bring down the quantity of wheat rather than the quantity of pale malt.

You can also play around with the spicing to achieve different flavors. Some notable examples of the style include other spices and herbs. For example, chamomile will impart a gentle floral character. Grains of Paradise or White Pepper will bring out peppery notes that work well with the Belgian yeast strain we've selected.

If you become confident brewing Witbier, you may want to try adding a fruit of your choice to the primary fermenter. You'll need about 2 pounds (1 kg) of whichever fruit you plan to use. In order to sterilize the fruit, simply place it in a mesh bag and suspend it in the cooling wort for fifteen minutes prior to whirlpooling. Then add the fruit (still in the mesh bag) to your primary fermenter. This is most

Grains of Paradise contain the peppery seeds you can use for Witbier.

effectively done with berries, which have the advantage of breaking down more readily than stone fruit. That said, you could easily use diced mango or peach.

If you're looking to do research on the style that goes beyond Hoegaarden and Celis White, you could examine the products of some of the Belgium-influenced breweries in North America.

These wild chamomile flowers are not just for tea.

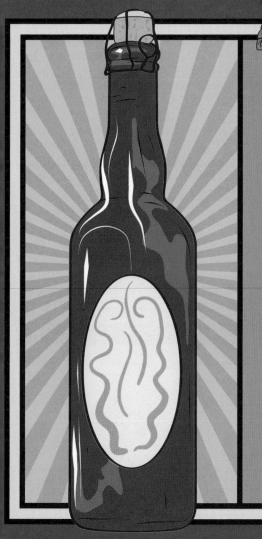

For instance, Unibroue's Blanche de Chambly is an excellent Canadian example with subtle spice and citrus notes, and it is almost universally available.

Large brewers have had success with Witbier as well. Blue Moon is an example that really benefits from adding a slice of orange. Coriander and orange peel are present, yet they are subtle so as to appeal to the widest possible audience, and the flavors are enhanced by the optional addition of fruit.

Fortunately, doing your home-work on Witbier is going to be pretty straightforward. Since its reintroduction in the mid-1950s, it has become a staple of the North American craft brewing scene. Nearly every brewery has played around with the style at some point.

White IPA

Although it's not a recognized style, one Witbier variation that is becoming popular is White IPA. Creating it involves the addition of significantly more hops at the end of the boil. Because it's predominantly an American variation, you would do well to use West Coast hops, which have a more citrusy flavor. Try increasing the coriander and orange peel slightly, and adding an ounce (28 g) of Columbus or Citra at the end of the boil. For extra kick, add another ounce to dry hop in the primary fermenter once fermentation is complete.

Chapter

5

California Common

California Common is America's original brew style, dating back to the pre-prohibition years. This unique half-ale, half-lager style pours a beautiful amber color, is slightly hoppy, but is balanced pleasantly by sweet crystal malts. California Common is a great gateway beer that you can serve to friends who are just discovering craft beer.

Gold-Rush Roots

To understand how California Common emerged as a beer style, you have to think back to the nineteenth-century settlers of the American West. Much of the expansion was driven by the promise of easy wealth. The Earp family, for example, famous for being law enforcers and outlaw hunters, would never have moved to Tombstone, Arizona, if the town hadn't been next to a silver mine. If the choice was becoming a sodbuster somewhere on the Great Plains or hunting buffalo for the railroad companies, staking a claim for gold in California must have seemed like a much better idea.

You can imagine that panning for gold was thirsty work. Luckily, a few brewskis were normally within arm's reach.

But the people who really made money during the California gold rush were those providing goods and services to the foolhardy miners. A town full of ambitious young men and a thirst powered by hard physical labor is a truly excellent place to start a brewery. By 1852, San Francisco had a population of 36,000 and about one saloon for every one hundred people. By 1854, California was growing hops and barley, and brewing had become big business. California Common was a license to print money.

The only problem in San Francisco for brewers was that it had a relatively warm climate for producing lager-style beer; but many of the brewers came from Germany, and they were in thrall to the new pale Pilsner pedigree. Nevertheless, they attempted to make it, but without refrigeration they lacked the cool conditions in which the new lager yeast thrived. Instead, the San Francisco brewers cooled their beer in shallow fermenting tanks, called "cooling ships," placed on rooftops. It's a practice still employed quaintly in parts of Europe.

The evening air blowing in off the Pacific ocean cooled the wort, producing clouds of steam that surrounded the brewery—hence the tag, "steam beer." This style was made

San Francisco's historic breweries took advantage of the winds coming off the ocean to cool the freshly boiled wort.

by many breweries before prohibition; however, only one brewery continued with it after prohibition. Anchor Brewing Company first brewed this beer back in 1896, and they've since trademarked the term "Steam Beer." It's for this reason that other versions of this style are now known as California Common.

Style and Profile

The defining characteristic of California Common is that it is fermented with lager yeast, but at a temperature more typical for an ale yeast. Fermentation temperature and yeast selection vary from brewery to brewery, but home brewers should buy WLP810 San Francisco Lager Yeast from White Labs or Wyeast's 2112 California Lager yeast, both of which are best fermented between 60 and 65°F (15.5 and 18°C).

BJCP Vital Statistics for California Common

A deep amber to light copper color, this brew is malty with some hints of caramel sweetness. The IBU range allows for a fairly bitter beer, equally as hoppy as your standard American Pale Ale.

OG: 1.048–1.054	BJCP = Beer Judge Certification Program	
IBUs: 30–45	**FG:** 1.011–1.014	
SRM: 10–14	**ABV:** 4.5–5.5%	

What's it Like?

Just some of the commercial beers in this style are: Anchor Steam, Southampton Steam Beer, Flying Dog Old Scratch Amber Lager.

TYPICAL HOPS USED:
Northern Brewer.

TYPICAL MALTS USED:
Pale ale malts with small additions of roasted or crystal malt.

Another hallmark of the style is the Northern Brewer hops. This variety was originally developed as a dual-purpose hop, suitable either for bittering or aroma. It produces woody, earthy, and slightly minty notes. To be faithful to the California Common style, it's best to avoid using hops with citrus or pine aromas. Hop varieties used in many West Coast beers didn't exist in the nineteenth century. Here, we're producing something of a hybrid anyway, but although we'll have between 30 and 45 IBUs—fairly bitter for a lager—the higher rate of hopping works well with the esters that our yeast produces.

Our beer will be medium amber to light copper in color, and whatever malt character there is will be provided by toasted or caramel malts. Conditioning at 50°F (10°C) for three to four weeks after fermentation will help clarify the beer. Since you will not have the ability to completely filter your beer at home, a long conditioning process will help to produce a beer that is far more pleasant to look at.

Without the aid of a time machine, it's difficult to imagine what California Common really tasted like over one hundred years ago. Even if we had the exact recipes today, it would be difficult to reproduce an exact nineteenth-century version, since ingredient quality and production methods have changed and improved. This is why modern interpretations of the style are compared to Anchor Brewery's classic version.

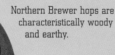

Northern Brewer hops are characteristically woody and earthy.

California Common—The Recipe

California Steamin'

Malt

LBs	OZ	KG	MALT TYPE
1	11	0.765	American Two-Row Pale Malt
0	4	0.113	Crystal 40L

	SPECIFIC GRAVITY	PLATO
Original Gravity	1.053	13.1
Final Gravity	1.016	4.1
Yeast Attenuation	69%	
Color	8 SRM, Gold to Copper	
Batch Size	1 Gallon (just under 4 L)	
Mash Efficiency	75%	

Hops

USE	TIME	OZ	GRAMS	VARIETY	AA
Boil	60 mins	0.125	3½	Northern Brewer	8.5%
Boil	15 mins	0.1	2¾	Northern Brewer	8.5%
Boil	5 mins	0.1	2¾	Northern Brewer	8.5%

IBUs	36
ABV	4.9%
ABW	4%

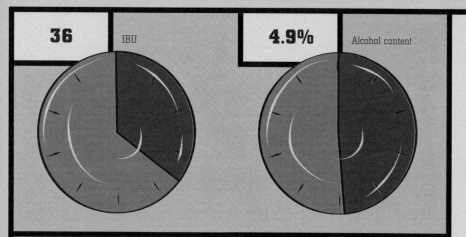

36 — IBU

4.9% — Alcohol content

top to bottom, as befits the recommendations of the BJCP.

We'll use a California Common yeast for this beer because it suits the fermentation temperature. A lager yeast that will ferment at the bottom range of ale fermentation temperatures is important for getting the flavor right.

California Common Brewing Method

1. Mash at 150 to 154°F (66 to 68°C).
2. Boil for sixty minutes.
3. Cool and ferment at 62 to 65°F (16 to 18°C).
4. After primary fermentation, condition the beer in your fridge for three to four weeks.

In this recipe, the majority of the fermentable sugars will come from Pale Malt, but there's a significant amount of Crystal 40L, which will provide color and some of the toasted character and grainy sweetness that helps to define the style. The hops are Northern Brewer from

Whole leaf vs. pellet, the choice is up to you.

NORTHERN
Brewer
Whole leaf hops
alpha 8.5%

Conditioning Your Beer

You'll notice this is a 1-gal. (4 L) recipe. While you might be able to get away with fermenting in a quiet corner of an air-conditioned basement or garage, you're eventually going to have to put your beer somewhere cooler to get it to condition properly. Since it might end up in your fridge, it's easier to use a 1-gal. (4 L) fermenter. If you want to try a 5-gal. (19 L) version, multiply the quantities by five.

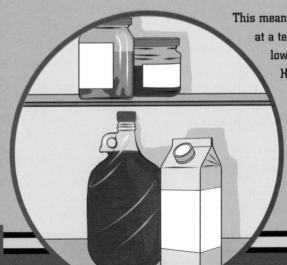

This means you'll be conditioning at a temperature that's slightly lower than recommended. However, one solution if you'd prefer to condition at the recommended 50°F (10°C) is to place the 1-gal. (4 L) fermenter into a cooler with chilled water. It will take some trial and error to discover

The "swamp cooler" is just one of many methods for controlling fermentation temperatures.

exactly how to get to that temperature, but with the use of ice packs it's possible.

In fact, controlling fermentation temperatures is one of the biggest improvements a home brewer can make. Since room temperature is typically above 70°F (21°C), even your ales are being fermented in overly warm conditions. In addition, fermentation produces heat, further raising the temperature of the fermenting beer by 5–10°F (-5 to -12°C), which can result in harsher alcohols and excessively fruity esters. A chest freezer with a digital temperature controller will help maintain a consistent temperature and allow for crash cooling at the end of fermentation. Dropping the temperature close to freezing and holding it there for a few days helps to clarify your beer.

Set it and forget it! With the aid of a chest freezer and temperature controller, you can produce commercial quality brews from the comfort of your own home.

Keepin' it Cool

California Common may well be your first foray into the world of lager fermentations, where temperature control is of utmost importance. Since a typical lager ferments between 50–55°F (10–13°C) and conditions around freezing for a week or two, you're going to need help in maintaining these frigid temperatures. For the home brew pro, you can buy a digital temperature controller and convert an old chest freezer or fridge into a fermentation chamber. If you're up for a little electrical project, you can purchase temperature controller model STC-1000 online for around $25, which will get you started.

Sample the Style

We recommend that you also explore the world of lagers at beer fests and your local bottle store, as there is much more out there than the mass-produced brands you were probably weaned on. Try some other beers that are made in approximately the same way as California Common. For example, the German-style Altbier and Kolsch are fermented with lager yeast at ale temperatures. They're both delicious.

Frederick Louis "Fritz" Maytag III

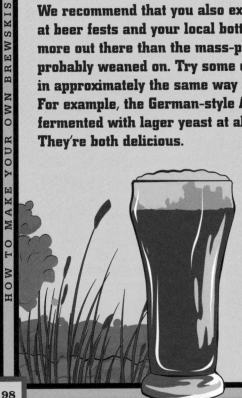

Still Steamin'

You remember the Anchor brewery we mentioned at the beginning of this chapter? After the repeal of prohibition, the revived Anchor Brewing Company suffered many hardships and was often near to bankruptcy. In 1965 Frederick Louis "Fritz" Maytag III purchased 51 percent of the brewery and later became the sole owner. Over time, Fritz was able to turn the brewery around and benefited from the beer renaissance of the 1980s. Today, he's regarded as one of the founding fathers of American craft brewing and you can still find him roaming around the annual Craft Brewers Conference, where he's treated with reverence.

Prohibition

Talk about alcohol abuse! Prohibition was instituted in the United States with the passing of the Eighteenth Amendment on January 16, 1919, effectively making it illegal to manufacture, sell, transport, import, or export alcohol within the United States. Even so, it was called the "Noble Experiment" for a reason, since it was a difficult law to enforce nationwide, and made illegal bootlegging a lucrative business. Only the largest breweries were able to survive by producing near-beer (low or no alcohol beer), malt syrup (for home brewers!), and other non-alcoholic beverages. The number of breweries fell from over 1,400 in 1910 to below 100 by 1930, with similar effects on the diversity of styles. Since prohibition's repeal on December 5, 1933 (with the passing of the Twenty-First Amendment), the number of US breweries has climbed back up to over 1,700.

What a sad sight it must have been as bar keepers were forced to dump their beer down the sewers.

CALIFORNIA COMMON

99

Chapter

6

Porter

Porter is a style of beer that has experienced a resurgence in popularity in North America as the result of craft brewing. It's a rich, satisfying, dark beer that doesn't have the same mildly burned character that is typical of its more popular cousin, Stout. Although you can enjoy it anytime, it's particularly good as a late autumn beer.

Pride of London

Instead of downing a six pack of light beer after a hard day, manual laborers once upon a time supped many pints and quarts of dark ale to quench their thirst. In the 1700s in London, England, Porter became the drink of choice in the poor working-class suburbs in the city's East End. Aside from quenching thirsts, this rich brew was seen as nutritious and was commonly accepted to be a drink of moderation.

The beer probably developed from an earlier style, called "brown beer." Because of the way that beer was brewed in those days, it would be delivered to taverns at different strengths and in different conditions.

Who would drink a six pack when you could have Porter instead?

Navvies

Porter was so popular among the railway workers in Britain in the nineteenth century that the Liverpool and Manchester railway company began to make deductions from the pay of the navigators, or "navvies"—as the builders of the railways were called—in order to provide them with brass tokens for food, so that they didn't spend all their money on Porter. It may have been calorically nutritious, but you can't live on beer alone.

When you walk into a bar nowadays, you ask for a specific brand of beer. The beer is drawn out of a single tap, and you know what you're getting. But to get a pint of Porter in Shoreditch in East London in the early eighteenth century, the barman would have drawn from several different casks behind the bar, probably partly to use up beer that was at the end of its "shelf" life. The resulting mix—usually served in a stoneware or pewter tankard, which masked the appearance of the liquid—was something that drinkers got to like.

Porter is usually served in a pint glass . . .

. . . but in the past, a pewter tankard would have been a classy serving vessel.

Doctor's Orders

During prohibition in the United States there were always ways to get your hands on beer. Porter was sometimes prescribed by doctors for patients with anemia and various other ailments—like severe, crippling, sobriety. This was entirely above board. In the case of the Narragansett Brewery in Rhode Island, a patent was issued by the government to allow them to continue production of their Porter, helping them get through a difficult period in US history for breweries.

Originally, this beer was known as "three threads," because the mix was usually drawn from three different casks. One brewer, Ralph Harwood, reputedly noticed the landlord of a pub called the Blue Last going through this elaborate practice, and decided to do the mixing in his brewery instead. The pub was frequented by market porters, so the brewery mix became known as Porter.

The proportions of the mix might change daily as the beer aged.

A Larger Scale

Other brewers soon followed Harwood's practice. In order to get the flavors right, brewers would leave the beer in vats for up to a year for conditioning. As you can imagine, brewing in a volume that would be profitable led to bigger and bigger vats. The largest was to be found at the Meux Brewery on London's Tottenham Court Road, and it held something like a million pints. It must have been a majestic sight. Then one day in October 1814, this giant vat burst and flooded a neighborhood, killing eight people. I think we can assume that the survivors suffered from fairly significant hangovers.

During the twentieth century, Porter waned in popularity to the point that it became a rarity, although some English brewers—

such as Fuller's of London and Samuel Smith in Yorkshire—have never stopped producing it. The current versions, though, are an evolution of the original style.

The resurgence in popularity of Porter is due in part to the huge number of American craft breweries that have chosen to brew it. This might be explained by the fact that the ale also harks back to the new settlers in the United States, who brought the style with them. Initially, the beer would have been imported from London, but breweries quickly sprang up in larger cities. The Redcoats might have gotten the boot after the Revolutionary War, but their beer was certainly welcome.

Hopefully, it never occurred to the brewers to go for a swim.

Style and Profile

Porter can range in color from dark brown to an opaque pitch black. It is different from that other black beer style, Stout, in that there is no roasted barley, and it therefore lacks the burned character that can be tasted in the majority of stouts. The BJCP style guidelines suggest that the final gravity for a Porter will be between 1.012 and 1.016, meaning that there is usually a significant amount of residual sugar after fermentation. This sweetness is used to great effect, especially by North American brewers, who will use the sugar to bolster other malt flavors like chocolate or coffee within their beer.

BJCP Vital Statistics for Porter

Porter may vary from moderately to aggressively bitter due to the use of hops. Because it will be either dark brown or black, color choice has merely to do with opacity. It should be full bodied with notes of roast and chocolate. Some booziness is acceptable, even in low-alcohol versions.	**OG:** 1.048–1.065	BJCP = Beer Judge Certification Program
	IBUs: 25–50	**FG:** 1.012–1.016
	SRM: 22–35	**ABV:** 4.8–6.5%

The malts used in Porter are fairly standard from brewery to brewery. Typically, Black Patent Malt, Carafa, Chocolate Malt, or Coffee Malt are preferred. It's not unusual to see some combination of these malts in a Porter recipe. Because of the way they are kilned, they will provide a roasted flavor, as well as some bitterness. Sweetness in a Porter comes from the addition of Crystal Malt.

There is a great deal more variation between breweries when it comes to choice of hops. Typical of the divide between European and North American brewers, hop choice is influenced by tradition and location. Many English brewers prefer traditional English hops, such as Goldings and Fuggles.

Sourness

Originally, because Porter contained some older beer in the mixture, there was a certain amount of sourness to it. This was usually due to wild yeast or the development of acetic acid. If you brew the recipe the way we've laid it out, you can avoid this almost entirely. Very small amounts of sourness are stylistically and historically accurate.

The specialty grains to the left make their way from a fairly light crystal malt through coffee, chocolate, and black patent malt.

Porter—The Recipe

Old London Style

Malt

LBs	OZ	KG	MALT TYPE
9	0	4	American Two-Row Pale Malt
0	8	0.227	Black Patent Malt
0	8	0.227	Chocolate Malt
1	8	0.680	Caramel Malt 30L

	SPECIFIC GRAVITY	PLATO
Original Gravity	1.059	14.5
Final Gravity	1.012	3.1
Yeast Attenuation	79%	
Color	33.6 SRM, None More Black	
Batch Size	5 Gallons (just under 19 L)	
Mash Efficiency	75%	

Hops

USE	TIME	OZ	GRAMS	VARIETY	AA
Boil	60 mins	1	28½	Nugget	13.0%
Boil	15 mins	1	28½	Willamette	5.5
Boil	5 mins	1	28½	Styrian Goldings	5.4%

IBUs	46.4
ABV	6.10%
ABW	4.88%

45 IBU

6.1% Alcohol content

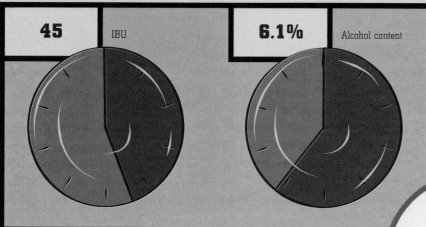

While our Porter is 6.1 percent alcohol, original London Porters would have ranged wildly because of the three threads method.

Fuggles gives a pleasing earthy character, but in this recipe we have chosen to use aroma hops. Willamette is an American variant of Fuggles, with an aroma that is both fruitier and more floral. Styrian Goldings is a Slovenian Fuggles variation, giving a slightly spicier character. Try substituting Fuggles for either aroma hop addition. You might also like to work the word Fuggles into daily conversation. It's fun to say. Fuggles.

Porter Brewing Method

1. Mash at 152 to 154°F (66 to 68°C) for sixty minutes.
2. Boil for sixty minutes.
3. Cool and ferment at 62 to 68°F (16 to 19°C) with Wyeast 1056 American Ale.

For this recipe, we have chosen a fairly light Crystal Malt variety, as the majority of the color will come from the dark malts. The SRM is 33, which is nearing the upper limit for the style. Our experience with robust American Porters is that brewers tend to push to the limit in terms of flavor and color.

Many new world hop varietals are the result of manipulating old world stock like Fuggles.

For bittering, the recipe uses an ounce (28 g) of Nugget hops. We've chosen Nugget because it is very high in alpha acids, so the desired amount of bitterness can be attained with a smaller quantity, making it cost effective. While Nugget can be used as an aroma hop to provide quite a heavy herbal character, when used for bittering, it will sacrifice most of that flavor. What remains should nicely compliment the Willamette and Styrian Goldings.

The yeast you use will depend on the character you want in your beer. Usually, for a beer that has this much dark malt, the malt and hop character should come through. Choose an American Ale yeast that ferments without adding a lot of flavor to the beer. If you want more of a fruit character, you can use a London Ale yeast, which will give you a character that's more similar to English Porters.

Sweet Fancy Molasses

One variation you might try for a winter Porter is to add molasses to your boil. It's a by-product of making sugar, and it has a number of interesting characteristics, including caramel, nuts, and fruit. Because it contains some non-fermentable material, the best thing to do is to add the molasses on top of the regular recipe and increase the boil time by thirty minutes. It may need to sit in bottles for a couple of weeks longer than the usual recipe, but the added complexity is worth it.

Adding a pound of molasses will take your porter closer to 7 percent alcohol.

Coffee Porter

At some point, you might want to try making a Coffee Porter. It's a fairly popular variation on American Robust Porter. Coffee doesn't have the burned, acrid notes that you might get from roasted barley. You can layer the coffee flavor in the beer by making a couple of modifications.

First, halve the amount of Black Patent Malt and replace it with French Kilned Coffee Malt.

Second, buy half a pound (227 g) of freshly roasted coffee and have it coarsely ground. Choose whatever type of coffee you like, but it should be freshly roasted. After the boil, while you're whirlpooling your beer in the kettle, add the coffee grounds into the vortex. Because the wort isn't boiling, you get maximum coffee flavor without any added acridity.

Despite the presence of significant coffee flavor, we can't recommend drinking this for breakfast.

Chapter

7

IPA (India Pale Ale)

The IPA (India Pale Ale) is a classic British beer style, with an interesting story behind it. The modern American interpretation is typically higher in alcohol and more heavily hopped. The beer has proven to be one of the driving forces behind the craft beer revolution. IPA can range from a nice citrusy quaffer to a pleasantly bitter, punchy brew.

IPA (INDIA PALE ALE)

Passage to India

The British Isles have a rich and fruitful brewing tradition. Over the centuries, they've created a large number of beer styles. This is where the roots of IPA (India Pale Ale) lie.

In order to understand why the style exists, it helps to know a little bit about the East India Company. From the mid-eighteenth century, the London-based global trading company ruled large areas of India. It managed to do this for about one hundred years, but in order to do this a large standing army was needed.

The soldiers' rations included about a gallon (4 L) of beer per day. Beer is a great source of Vitamin B, and it was considered safer

Traditional English hops include East Kent Golding, Fuggle, and Bramling Cross, and are more mellow than their American counterparts.

than the local drinking water. There was also the issue of morale if the men went without their liquid rations. "I don't know what effect these men will have upon the enemy, but, by God, they frighten me," said the Duke of Wellington, who commanded in India for a time. Clearly, these were people you wanted to keep happy. The trade of an empire was dependent on men with muskets—and a taste for beer.

The problem was that India was extremely hot and, at that time, before refrigeration, a difficult place in which to make beer. Growing hops and barley might have been feasible in the cooler regions of the subcontinent, but it would certainly have taken a long time to get right. So it was decided to keep the soldiers happy by shipping their beer out to them from England.

A Beer Abroad

In the late 1700s, trade ships traveled from India to England full of spices and silks, and would normally return to India empty. George Hodgson of the Bow Brewery took advantage of cheap shipping rates to export beer to India. By 1800, 9,000 barrels of beer per year were being shipped to India.

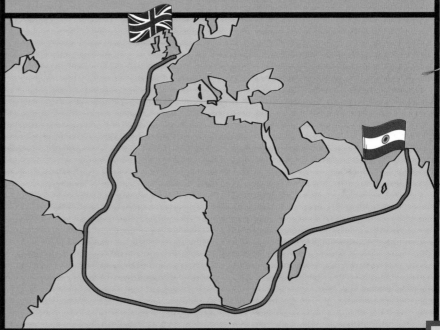

However, this was fraught with problems as well. It was long before the Suez Canal was engineered, so ships had to go around the horn of Africa and across the Indian Ocean. Even a fast ship could take four months to reach India, so beer would often arrive spoiled or sour.

The answer was India Pale Ale. There is debate about its history, such as when it was first developed and what it might have tasted like. If it weren't for the government records and the newspapers of the day, we wouldn't have a date for the advent of the style. Fortunately,

Soldiers were a thirsty bunch, with a fondness for beer that reminded them of distant home.

brewers have always appreciated the art of advertising.

IPA was designed to be less susceptible to spoilage on long journeys by being higher in alcohol (difficult for bacteria to survive in), highly hopped (hops are chock full of natural antiseptic properties), and having a lower final gravity (less residual sugar for damaging bacteria to eat and thrive in). Thus, the beer arrived with British soldiers the way that it was meant to be.

Another important development that led to the production of IPAs were the advances in the malting process. Previously, malt was kilned over an open wood fire, which resulted in smoky malts of a darker color and, in turn, brown ales. With the Industrial Revolution developing in England in the eighteenth century, coke (derived from coal) as a heat source led to increased steel production and new malting equipment. Malt could now be kilned by an indirect heat source, resulting in paler malt with fewer smoky characteristics. This new malt produced lighter-colored wort with more easily fermented sugars. Pale ales were considerably drier and less sweet than the Porters being produced at the time.

Double / Imperial IPA

Hopheads, in their search for extreme bitterness and aroma, have taken to enjoying bigger and bigger IPAs. Some of these go higher than 9 percent alcohol and 110 IBUs. They can be delicious, but do have the side effect of feeling as though you've been beaten about the head and neck with a giant hop cone.

Style and Profile

What does all this have to do with American IPA, you may ask? Well, the American beer revolution has led to the production of numerous styles with intense flavors. American IPA is one of the places where this is most prevalent because of the number of hop varieties that have sprung up on the West Coast. Now being produced in countries around the world is an American style of IPA, independent from the classic British example.

BJCP Vital Statistics for IPA

The IPA covers a wide color spectrum, ranging from gold to copper. Malt flavor is typically low, as both hop bitterness and flavor are at the forefront. American hops give citrus, resin, pine, floral, and fruity aroma and flavor notes. Bitterness may linger, but should not be too harsh.	**OG:** 1.056–1.075	BJCP = Beer Judge Certification Program
	IBUs: 40–70	**FG:** 1.010–1.018
	SRM: 6–15	**ABV:** 5.5–7.5%

A modern English IPA is generally lower in both alcohol and IBUs compared with an American IPA, and uses classic English hops such as East Kent Goldings and Fuggles.

An American IPA is an exercise in nerve straining, puckering bitterness, and concentrated hop aromas. If English IPA is the Beatles, then American IPA is Metallica at their hardest.

As you can see, the BJCP guidelines for the style go up to 70 IBUs. American craft brewers don't care for arbitrary limits, however, since some popular examples will range as high as 90 IBUs.

Locally Grown

The stars of the show are the hops being used. Some of the more popular US hop varieties include:

- US Cascade: The hop variety that put American craft brewing on the global map. It was first released in 1972 and was the first commercially accepted American-bred aroma hop. The Cascade hop has citrusy, flowery, and grapefruit aromas and flavors.

- US Centennial: Cascade's bigger and stronger brother, Centennial is higher in alpha acids (bittering potential) and packs a whopping citrus punch.

- US Simcoe: A relatively new bittering hop (released in 2000) with big piney and resiny flavors and aromas.

- US Crystal: Crystal hops are very popular in the craft brewing industry and are known for pungent spicy and flowery aromas.

- Together, Cascade, Centennial, Chinook, and Crystal are known as "C" hops.

For some, it's an acquired taste; but once you're hooked, you'll become a freakin' hop zombie, stopping at nothing to find more and more IPA.

IPA—The Recipe

Beautiful Gold

Malt

LBs	OZ	KG	MALT TYPE
10	0	4.50	American Two-Row Pale Malt
1	4	0.567	Caramel 40L
0	8	0.227	Munich Malt

	SPECIFIC GRAVITY	PLATO
Original Gravity	1.065	15.9
Final Gravity	1.016	4.1
Yeast Attenuation	74%	
Color	9 SRM, Gold to Copper	
Batch Size	5 Gallons (just under 19L)	
Mash Efficiency	75%	

Hops

USE	TIME	OZ	GRAMS	VARIETY	AA
Boil	60 mins	1.5	42½	Chinook	13.0%
Boil	15 mins	0.5	14	Cascade	5.5%
Boil	1 min	0.5	14	Cascade	5.5%
Boil	1 min	0.5	14	Centennial	10%
Dry Hop	7 days	1		Centennial	

IBUs	60
ABV	6.50%
ABW	5%

60   IBU

6.5%   Alcohol content

Too much caramel malt can overpower the hops. Balance in life, balance in beer.

IPA Brewing Method

1. Mash at 153°F (67°C) for sixty minutes.
2. Boil for sixty minutes.
3. Cool and ferment at 65–68°F (18–20°C).
4. Once primary fermentation is complete (three to five days), dry hop in primary for seven days.

With this recipe, you're going to get an IPA that's 6.5 percent alcohol and a light copper color. The Pale Malt adds balance to the actual fermentable material, but the addition of Caramel 40L Malt will provide sweetness and color. The Munich Malt will give the beer a very slight orange tinge and additional sweetness for a true IPA that demands some attention.

Creative License

The possibilities are endless when it comes to hop combinations. You can make substitutions as you see fit; just be aware that the quantity and alpha acid level of the hops added at the beginning of the boil will drive the IBUs in the finished product.

The Chinook hops that you're using for bittering are relatively neutral in flavor, and their alpha acids will isomerize completely into the beer. The real flavor here is going to come from the Cascade and Centennial hops, giving your beer a really powerful aroma of citrus and pine.

Dry Hopping Benefits

You'll get a special kick from the ounce (28 g) of Centennial that goes in during dry hopping. Dry hopping will add no additional bitterness to the beer; instead, it imparts the citrusy and floral aromas and flavors normally lost during the boil. Adding the hops after primary fermentation has occurred will ensure that none of these aromas are lost during the early stages of vigorous fermentation. Adding between one and two ounces (28 and 57 g) of hops per 5-gallon (19 L) batch will impart a moderate amount of hop aroma and flavor. Big "hop head" beer drinkers might add up to 5 ounces (142 g) at this point in the process. You'll have to play with the recipe to determine how hoppy you want it. Go for hops with low alpha acids to get the most out of the essential oils.

IPA often packs a proverbial fruit punch.

Whole leaf dry hopping may add to the clean-up, but it's worth it.

Black IPA or American Style India Black Ale— or Cascadian Dark Ale?

Porter + IPA = Hoppy Chocolaty Deliciousness. Try it, you'll like it.

It doesn't matter what you call it; these beers are tasty. Some beery people credit the work of Greg Noonan of the Vermont Pub & Brewery for creating the original Black IPA way back in the early 1990s (although some real sticklers will say it was being brewed as far back as the 1800s, when lighter kilned malts weren't available). However, it's only been in recent years that this style has enjoyed a resurgence and really taken off.

To move from a standard American IPA recipe to something resembling a Black IPA, try adding 10 to 12 ounces (283 to 340 g) of either chocolate malt or black malt to your brew. For added complexity, try a combination that includes some of the higher kilned crystal malts. These dark, highly roasted malts will impart notes of chocolate, coffee, and burned caramel to your IPA.

Now for Some *Serious* Research

The much darker malts bring an additional level of flavor to a beer that's already jam-packed with citrus and floral aromas, and will give you something to impress your friends with. The style is new enough that some of them won't have tried it before.

The way to decide how hoppy you want your beer is by doing some drinking research first. Some of the best commercial examples include AleSmith IPA, Bell's Two Hearted Ale, Stone IPA, Bear Republic Racer 5, Sierra Nevada Torpedo, and Dogfish Head's 60 Minute IPA.

If you're interested in playing with the varieties of hops used in our recipe, and you've found a beer that you like and you want to try to copy, you can probably find out what hops are used in that beer by contacting the brewery. Brewers are not as secretive as they once were about what goes in their beer.

If you really like a certain hop, why not try a Single Malt And Single Hop (SMASH) brew? There's no better way to showcase a certain hop's unique aroma and flavor profile. If you're interested in learning more about the history of IPA, pick up *Hops and Glory* by Pete Brown, which is the story of one man's obsessive quest to transport a cask of IPA from England to India by boat. Not only does it explain a lot about the origin of the style, it's hugely entertaining.

And you can drink while you read.

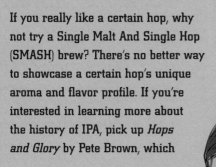

To Cellar or not to Cellar?

Beers, just like some wines, can improve with age. Beers higher in alcohol can mellow and actually transform over time. Store your beers in a cool, dark place, at consistent temperatures in the 50–55°F (10–13°C) range. Drink one immediately so that you have a reference point, and then another six months to a year later to see how it has aged. While some ardent hop heads argue fresh is best, it's up to you as to how you enjoy your beer.

Glossary

Adjunct

Any fermentable material not derived from barley malt. Most commonly includes corn, rice, wheat, and refined sugars.

Ale

A brew fermented at warmer temperatures (59–77°F or 15–25°C) using ale yeast. Ale yeasts are top-fermenting and are known for producing fruity esters. Common ale beer styles include Pale Ale, Porter, Stout, IPA, and Wheat Beer.

Attenuation

The degree to which the sugars in the wort were converted into alcohol and CO_2 by the yeast.

Blow-off

Replaces the typical airlock by running a piece of hose from the top of the fermenter into a bucket of sanitizer. A blow-off tube is less likely to clog and is best used at the beginning of fermentation.

Dry Hopping

Adding hops directly to the fermenter, typically once fermentation has slowed down, to impart hop aroma in the beer.

Hops

The flower of a climbing vine. Hops will impart bitterness, flavor, and aroma in the beer. Hops come in pellet form and as a whole flower.

IBU

International Bitterness Units are a standard measure of the concentration of bitter hop acids in your beer. Beers with fewer than 20 IBUs have a low amount of bitterness, while beers with higher than 40 IBUs would be considered to be quite bitter.

Krausen

Forms as fluffy foam at the top of the fermenter during primary fermentation. Consists of yeast, wort proteins, and hop matter.

Lager

A brew fermented at cooler temperatures (45–59°F or 7–15°C) using lager yeast. Lager yeast ferments slower than ale yeast, and settles to the bottom as fermentation completes. Common lager beer styles include Pilsner, Bock, and Dunkel.

Acronyms used in the tables in this book:

AA - Alpha Acids (see also pages 18 and 19)
ABV - Alcohol By Volume
ABW - Alcohol By Weight
OG - Original Gravity
FG - Final Gravity